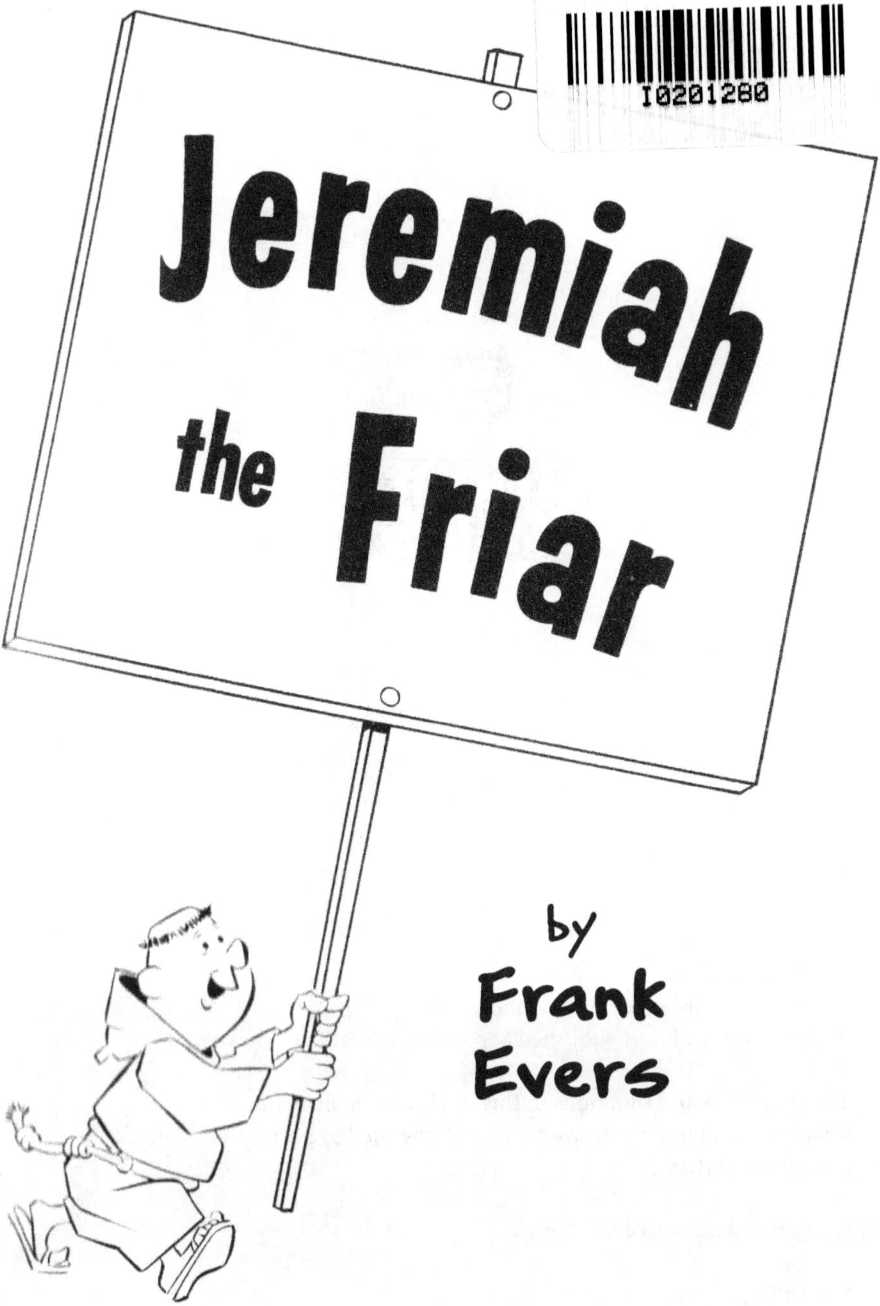
Jeremiah
the Friar

by
Frank
Evers

ABOUT COMICS | CAMARILLO, CALIFORNIA

Jeremiah the Friar
Originally published by Abbey Books, 1962
About Comics edition published September, 2018

The characters and situations in this work are wholly fictional and imaginative; do not portray, and are not intended to portray, any actual persons or parties.

Customized editions available

Send all queries to *questions@aboutcomics.com*

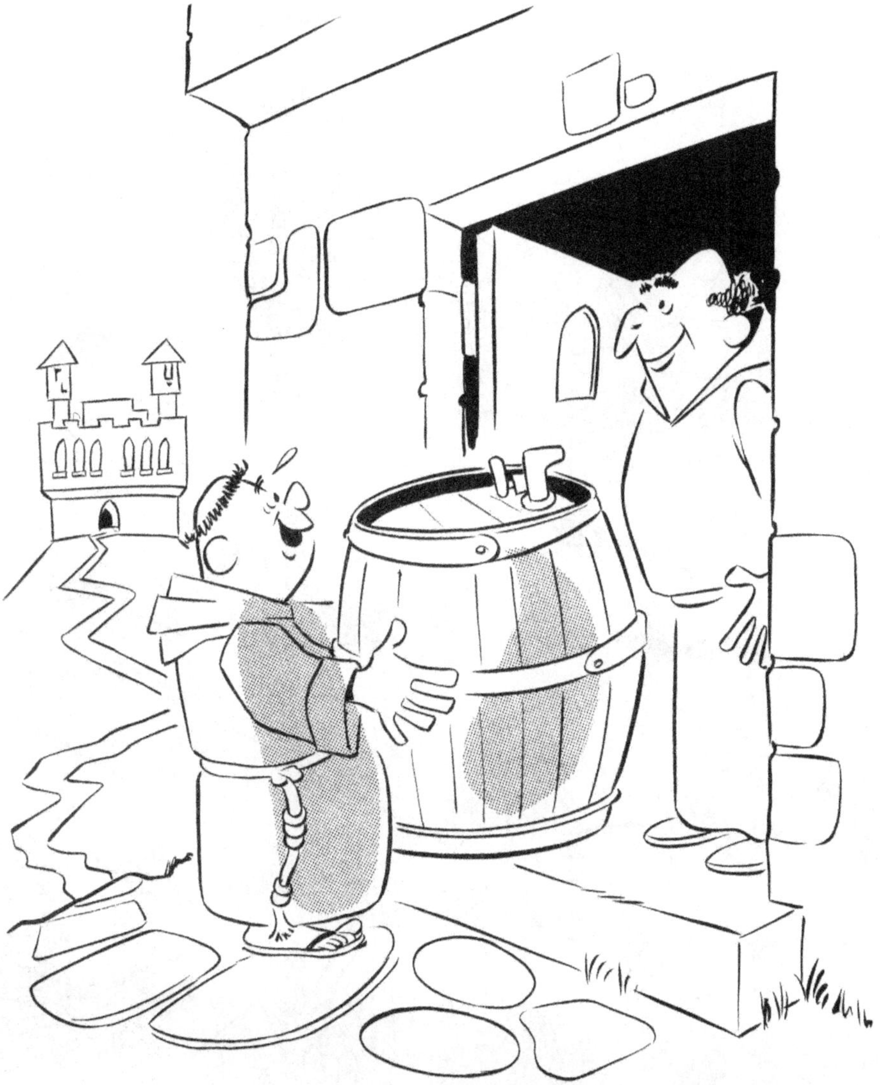

We've run short. Can you help us out?

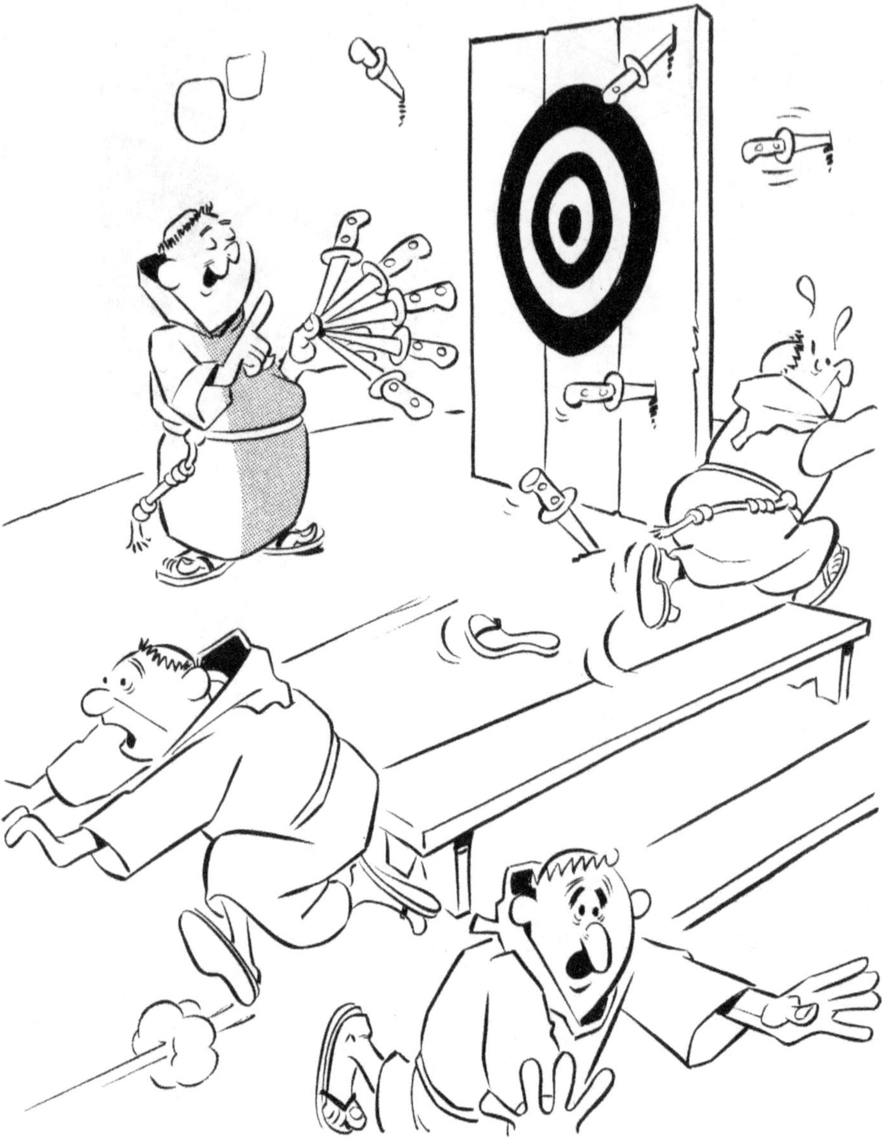

...And now may I have a volunteer.

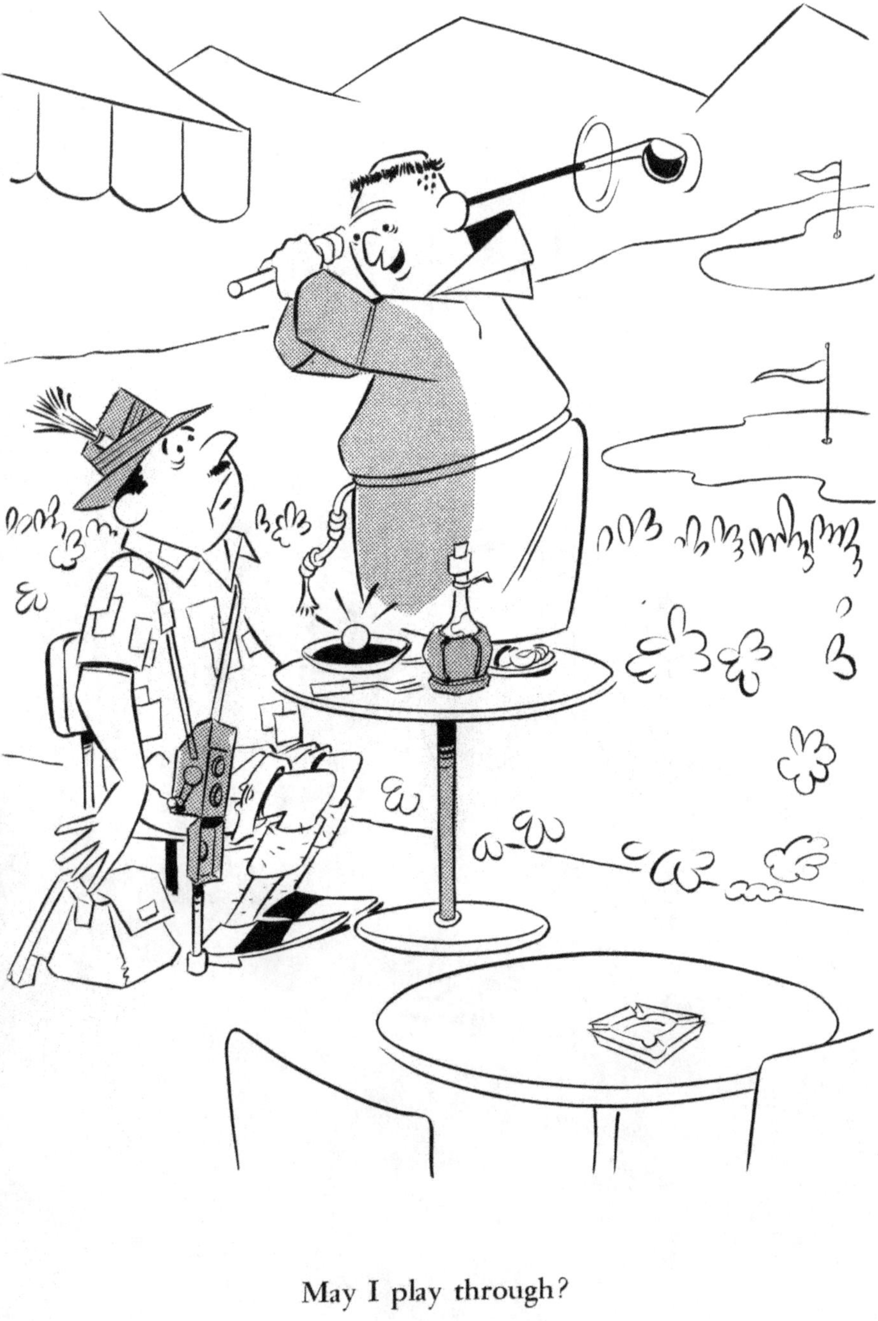

May I play through?

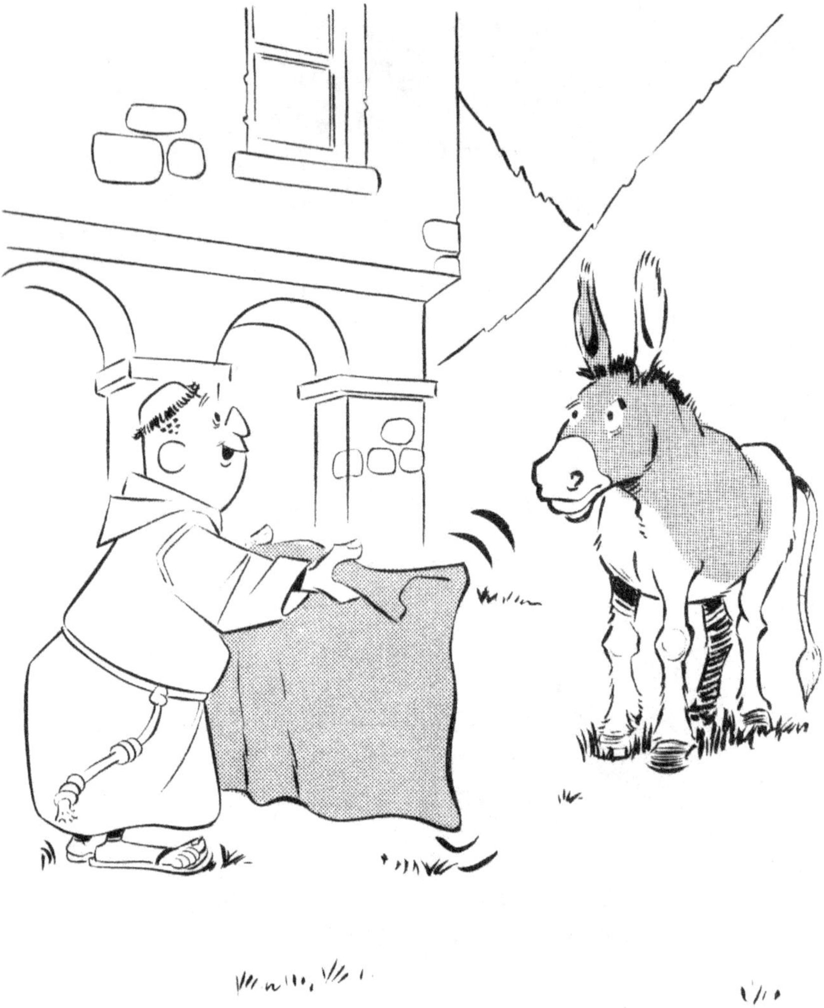

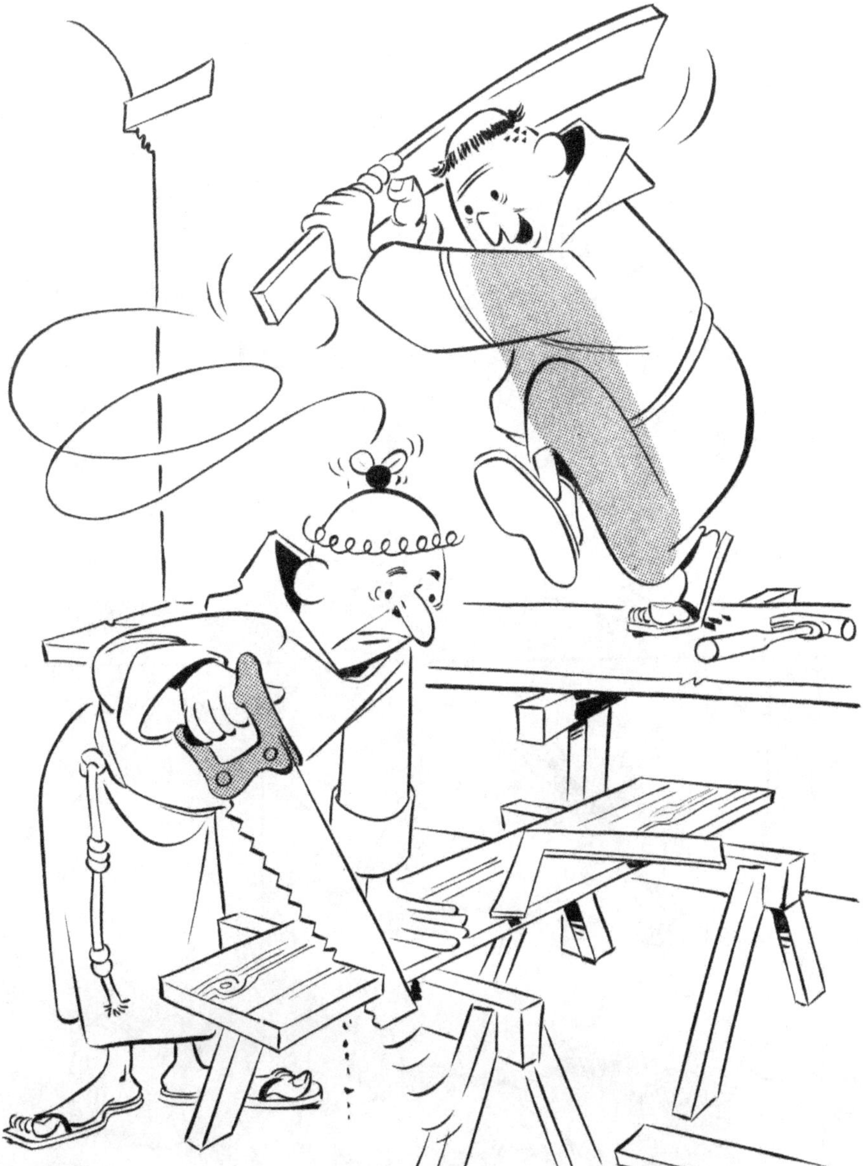

Hold it!

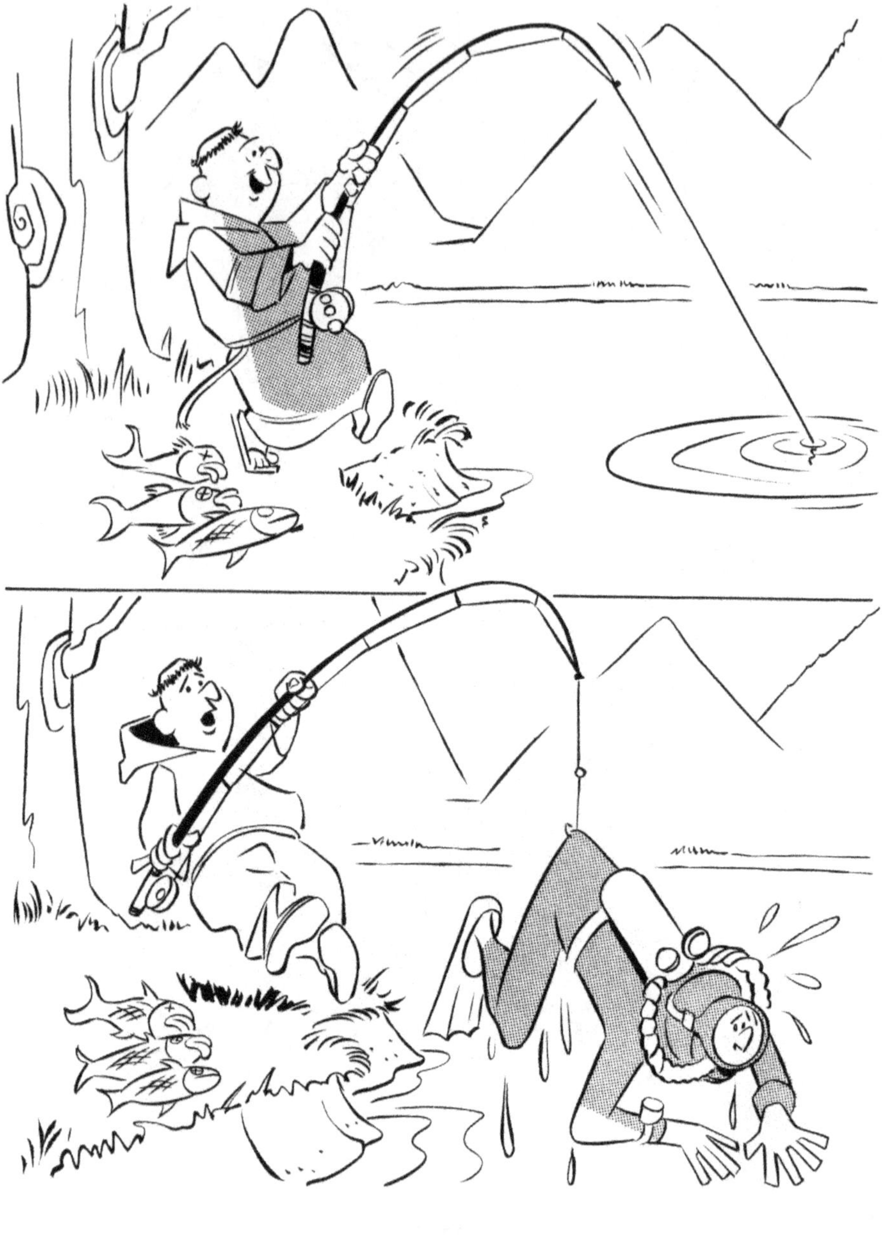

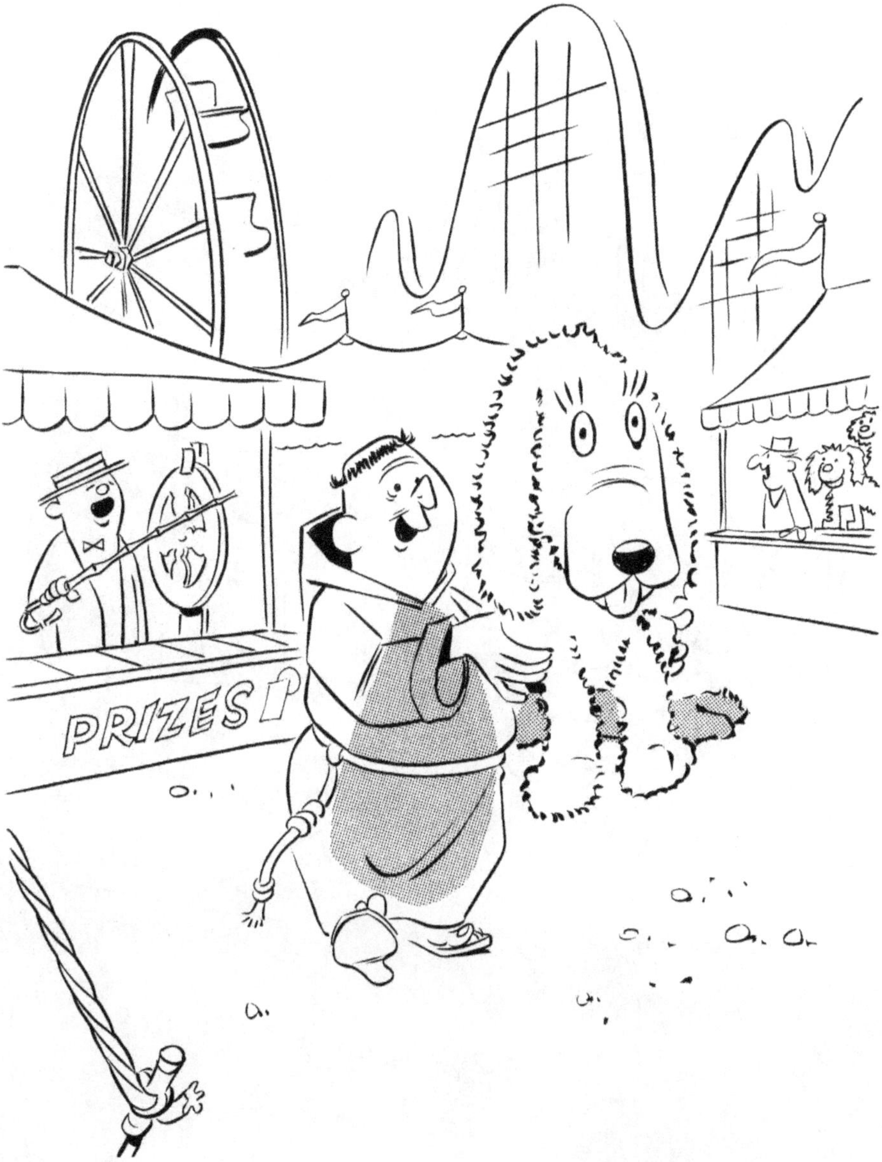
PRIZES

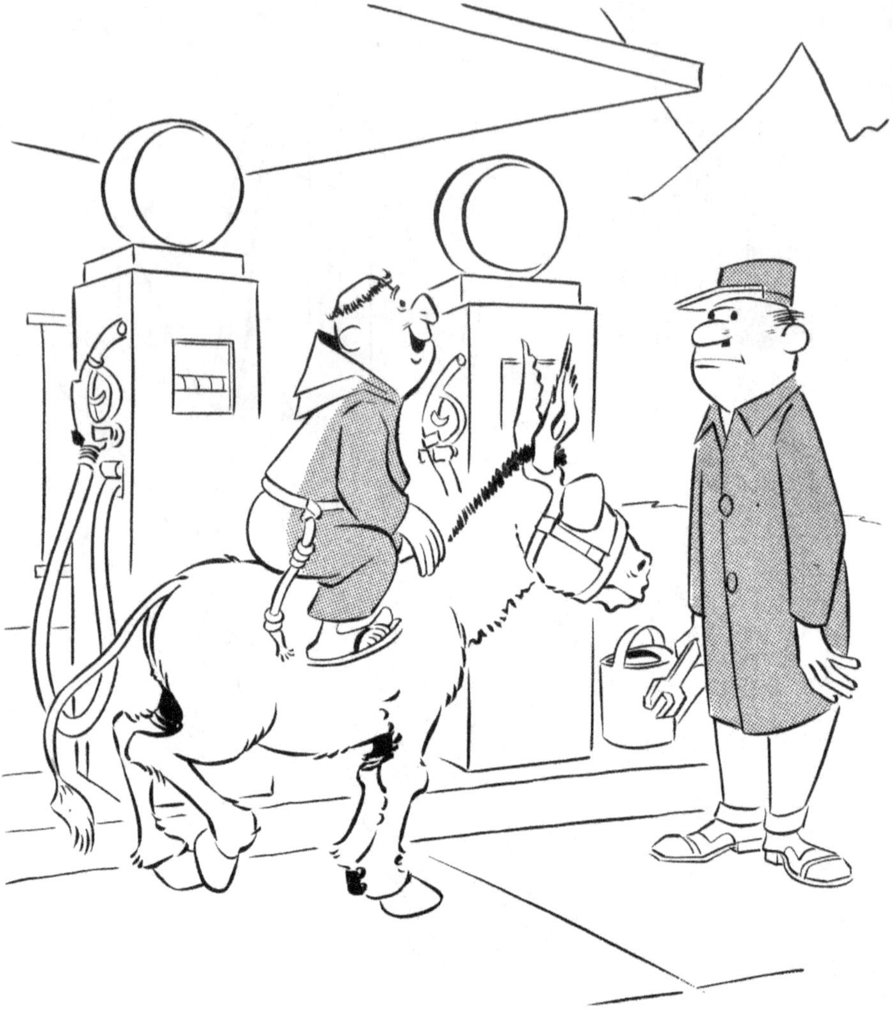

Fill 'er up... with water that is!

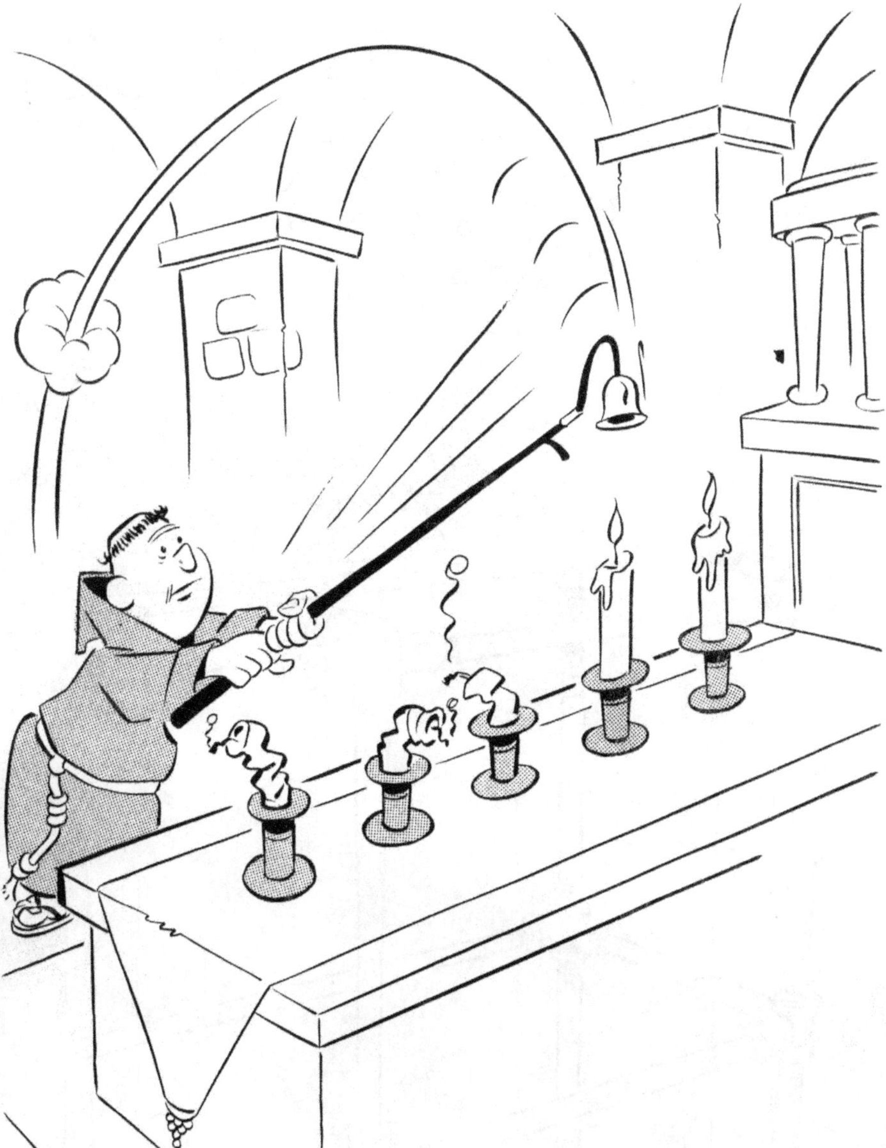

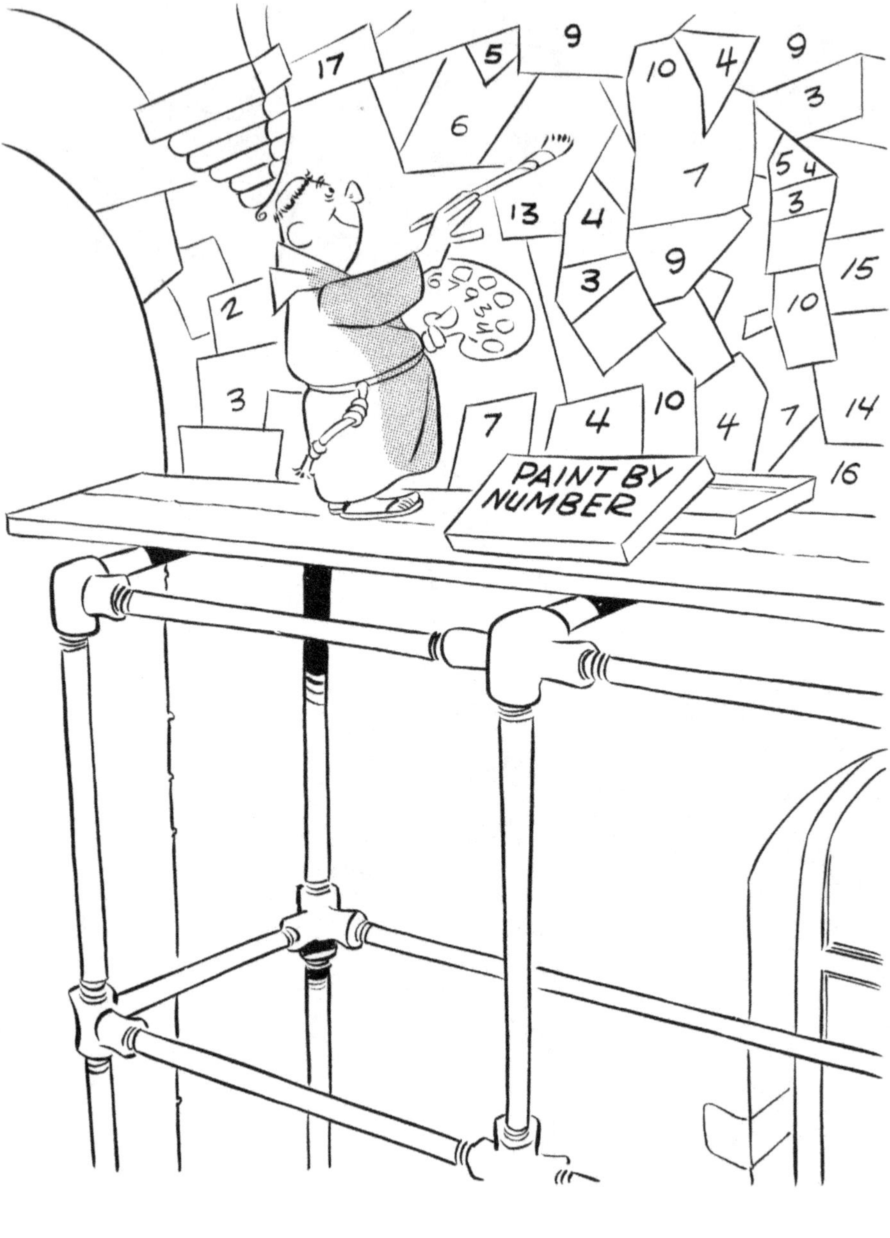
PAINT BY NUMBER

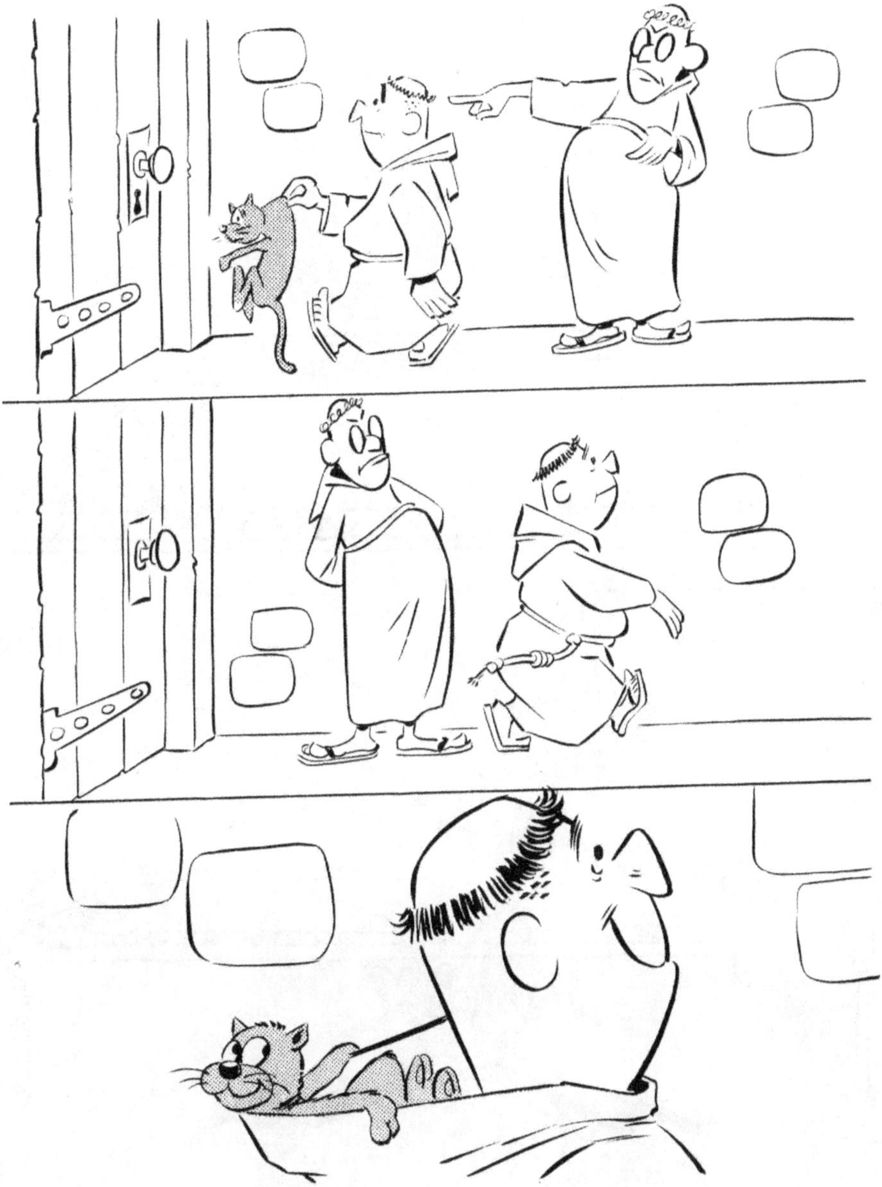

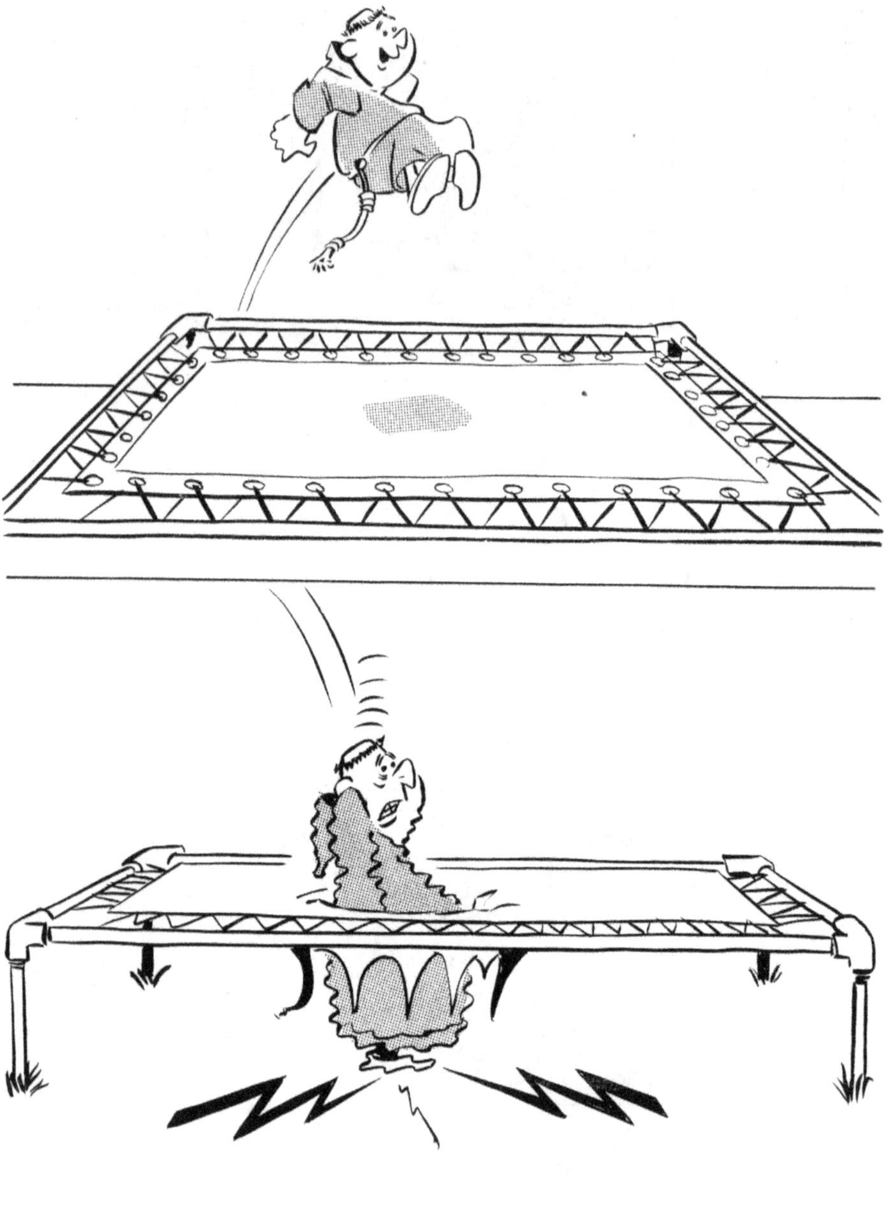

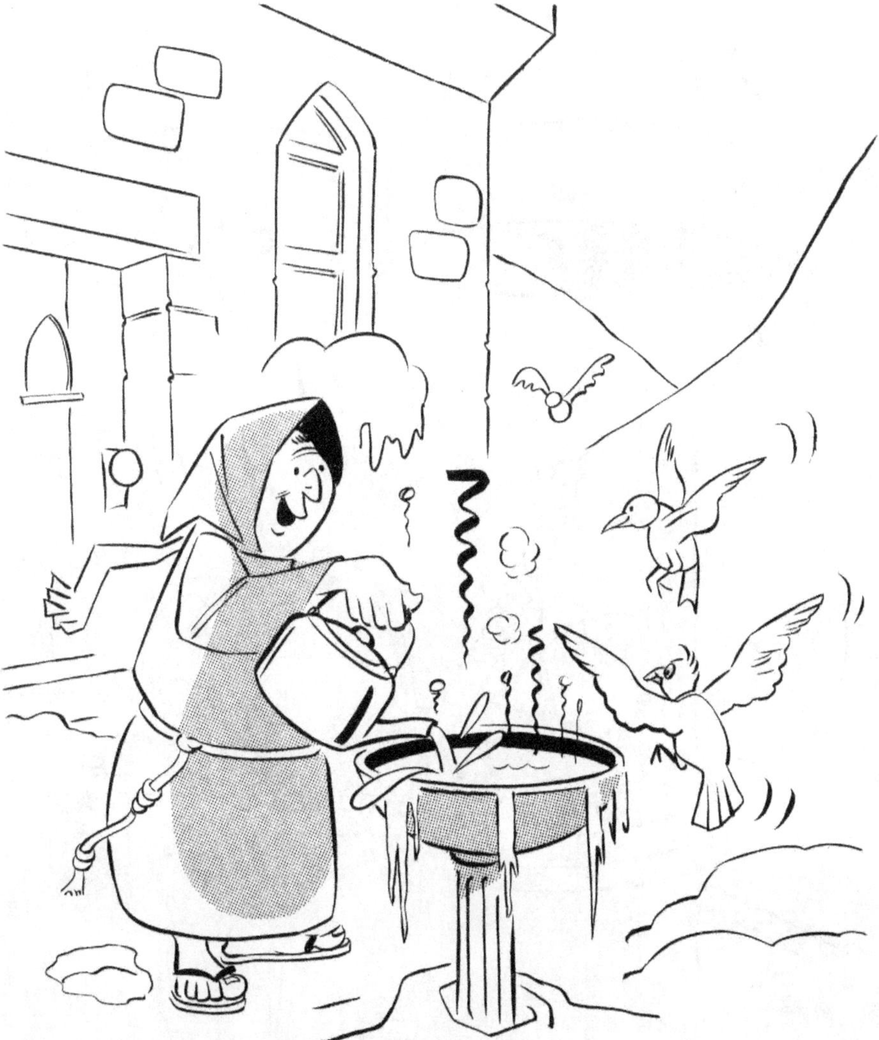

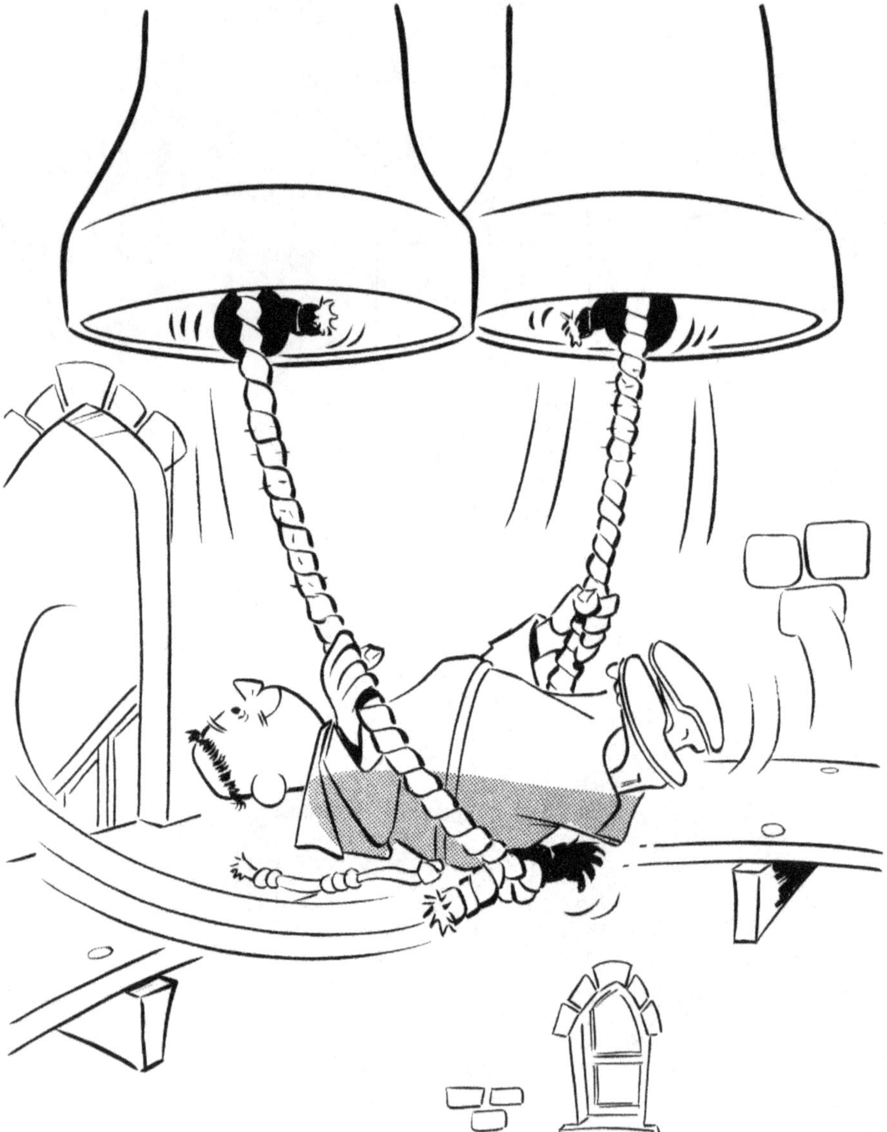

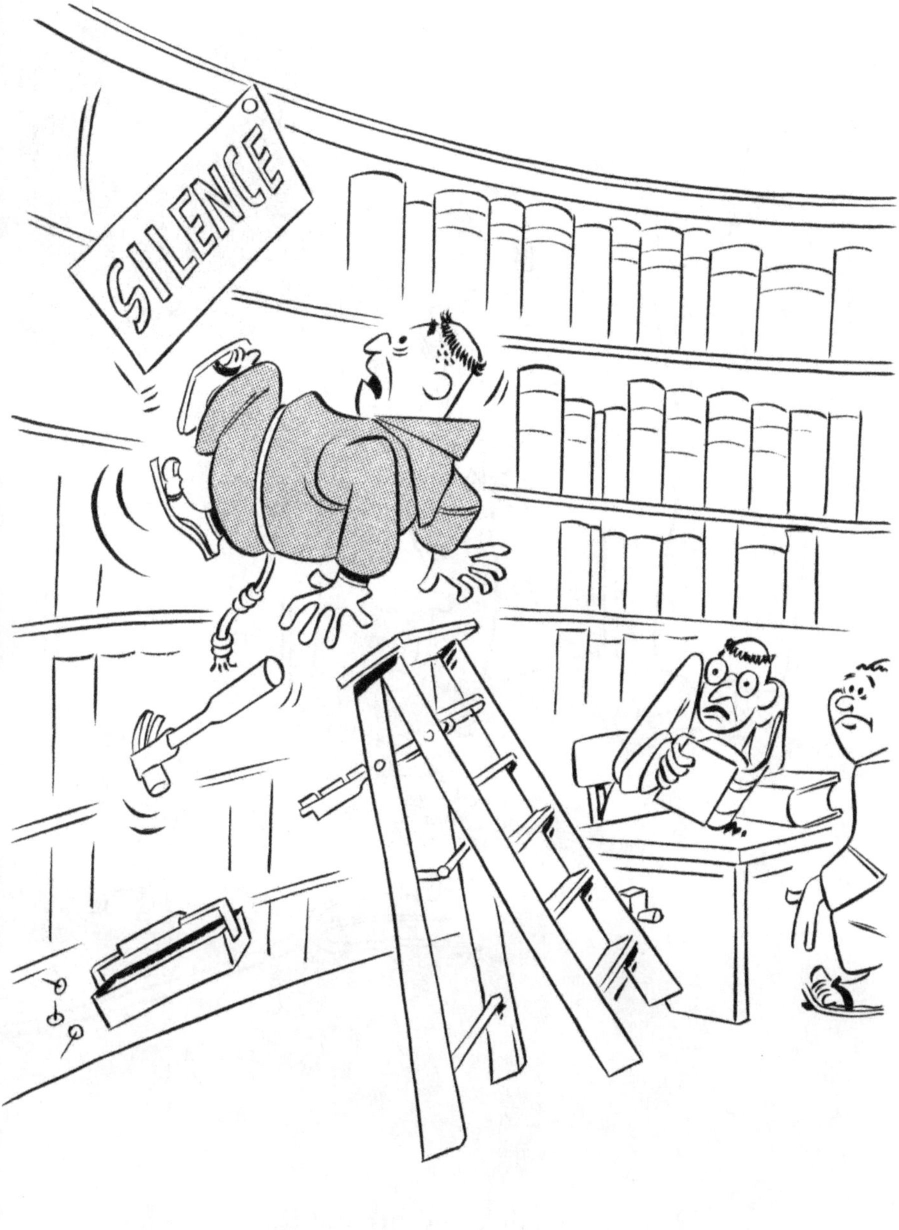
SILENCE

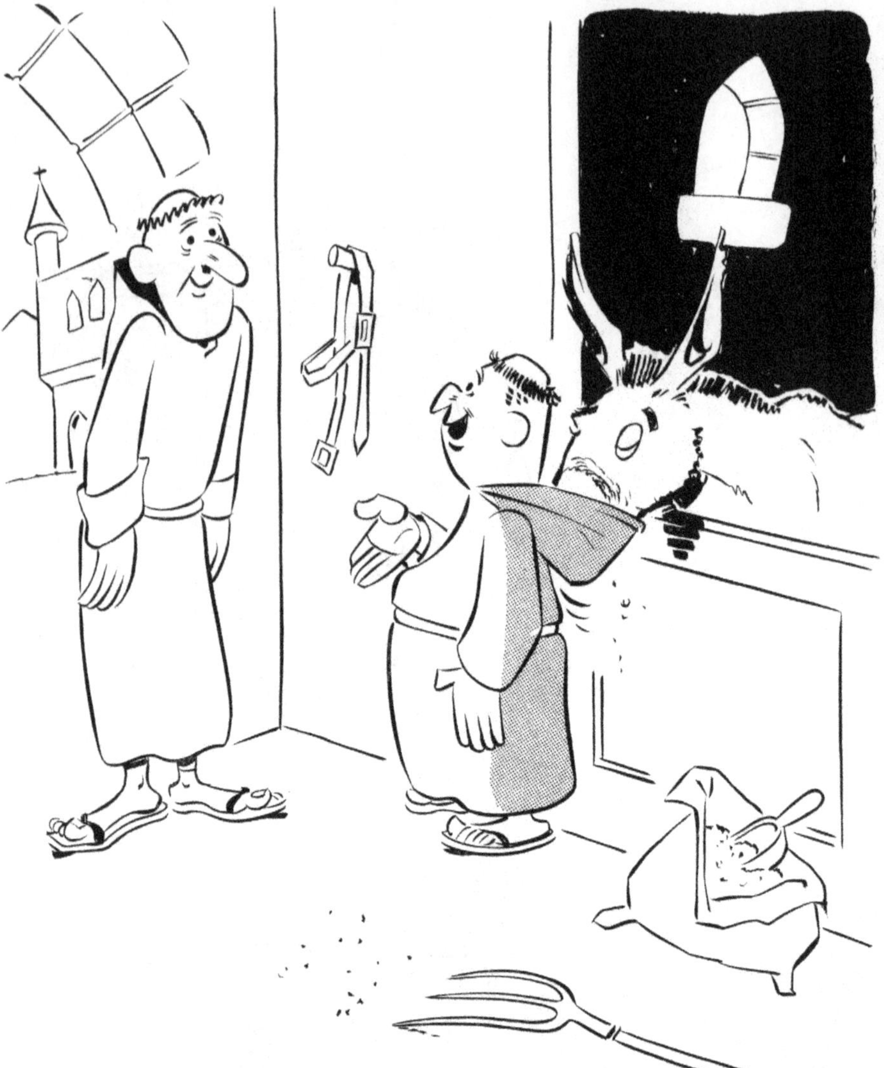

I couldn't find his feed bag.

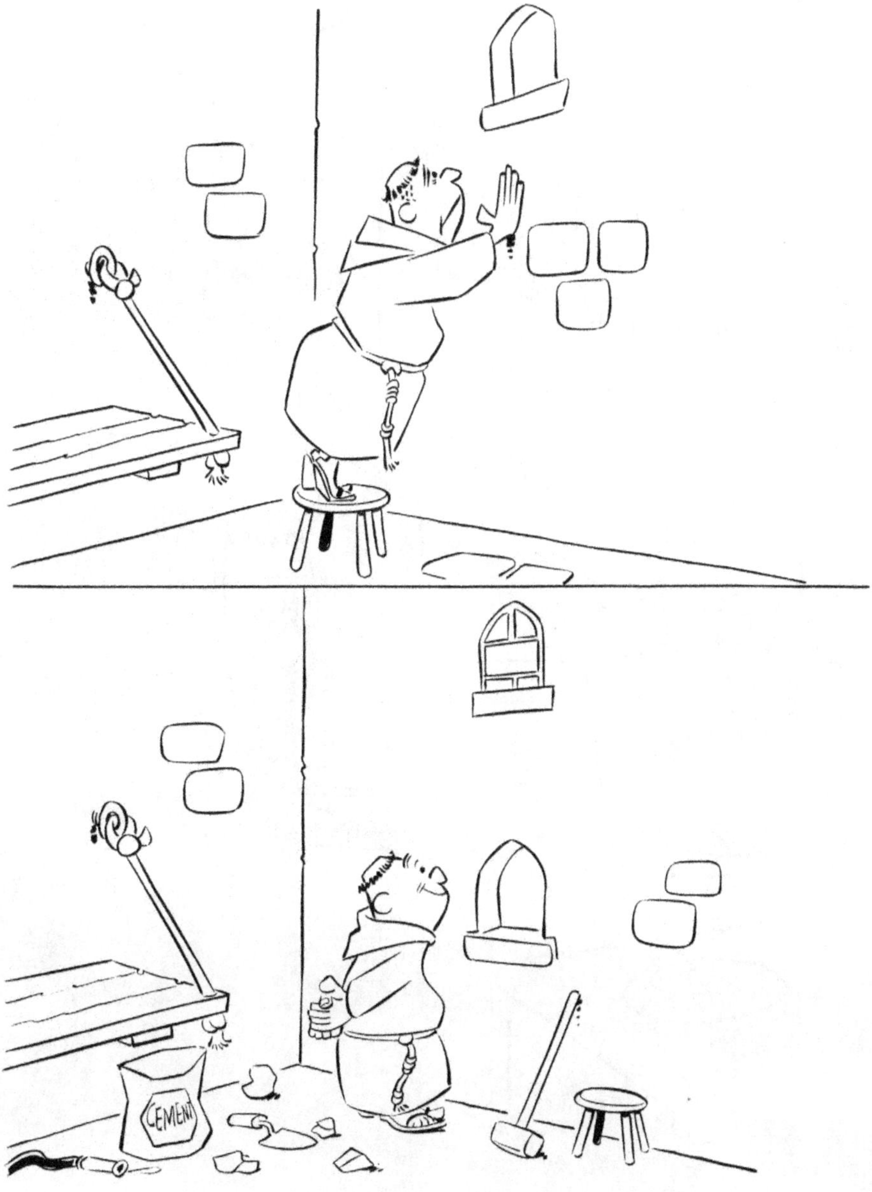
CEMENT

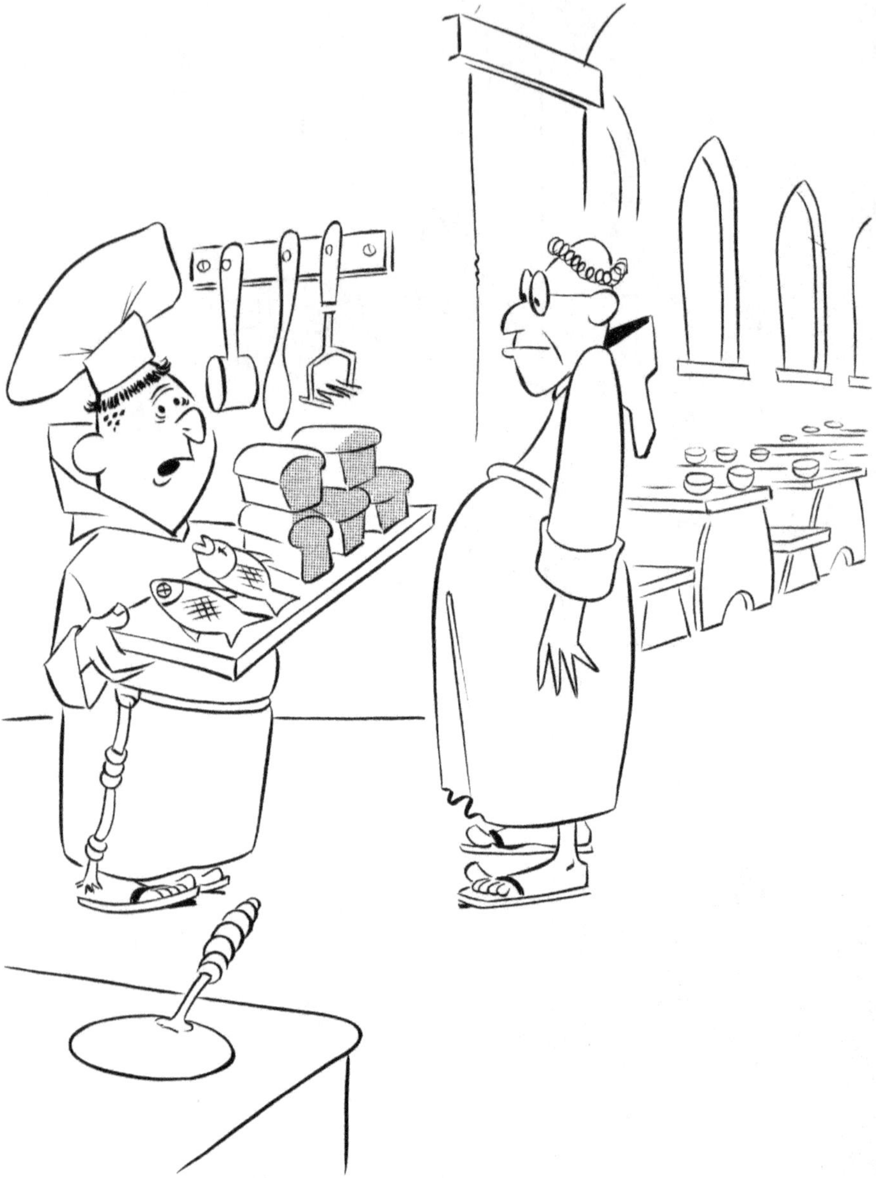

All we have left is five loaves and two fishes.

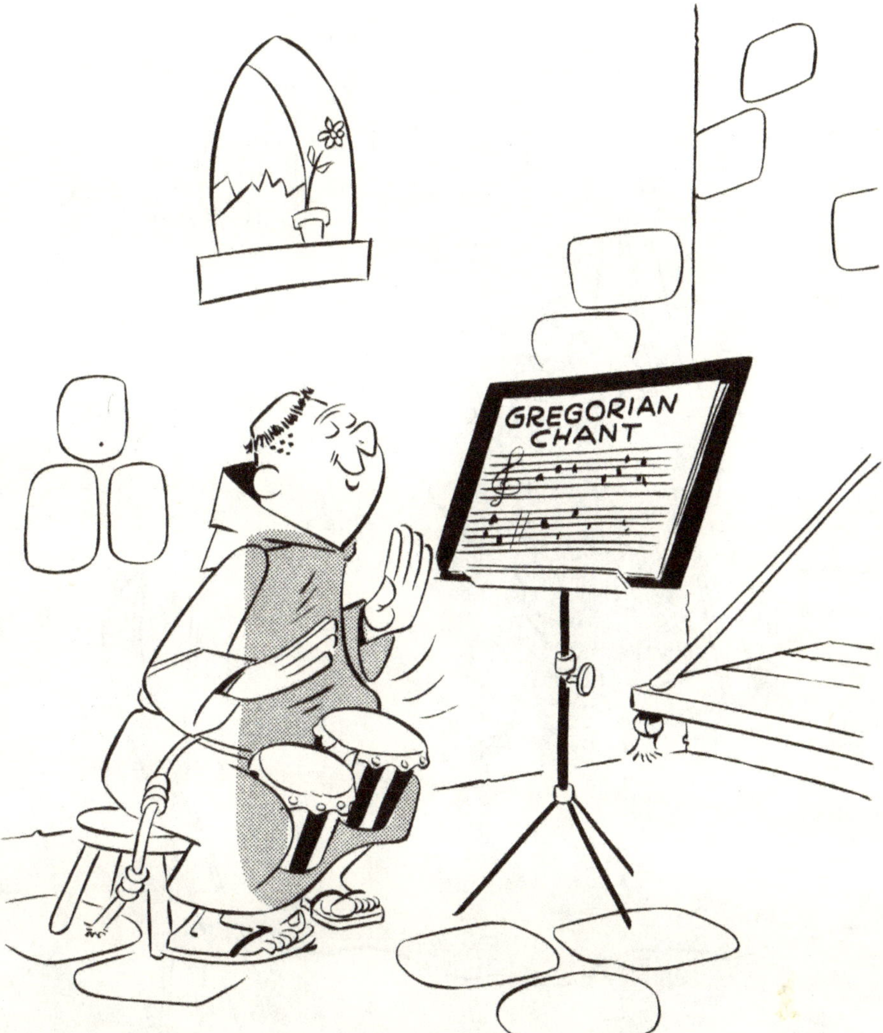
GREGORIAN
CHANT

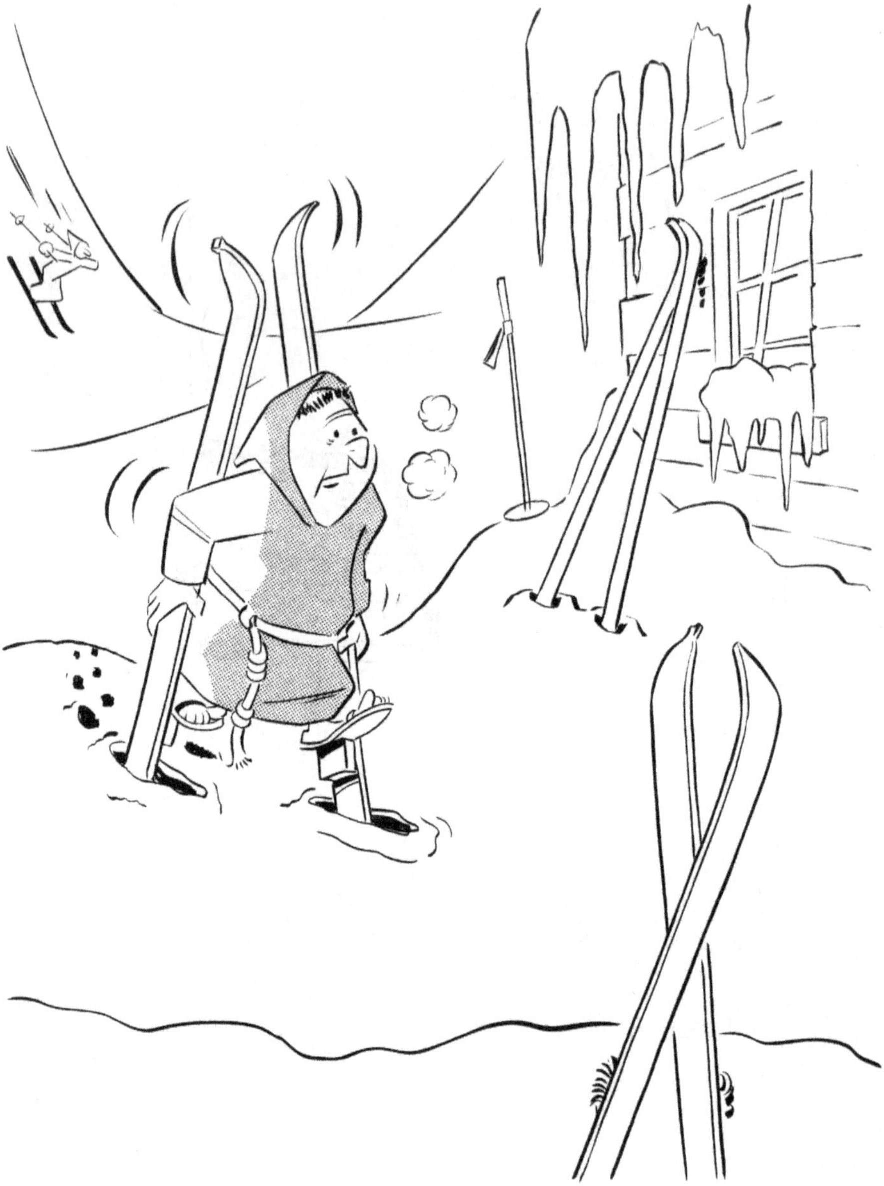

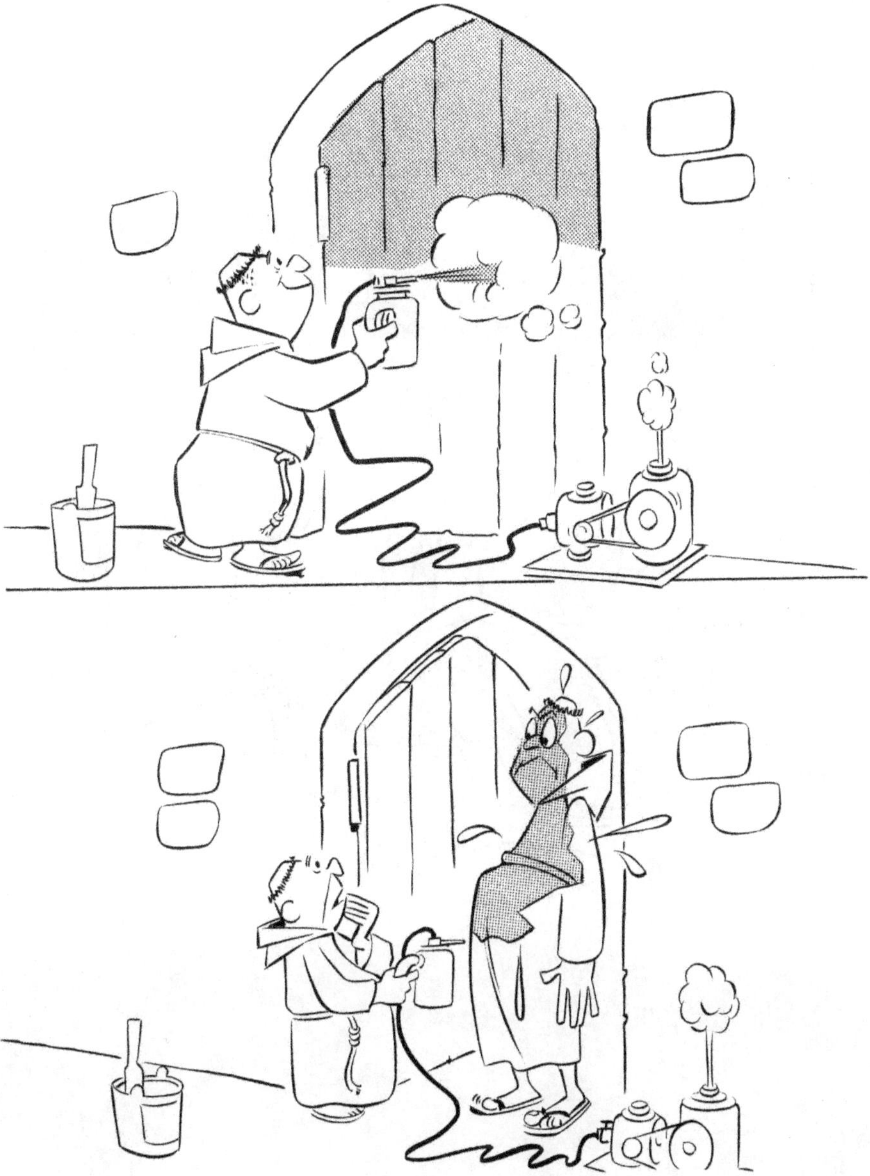

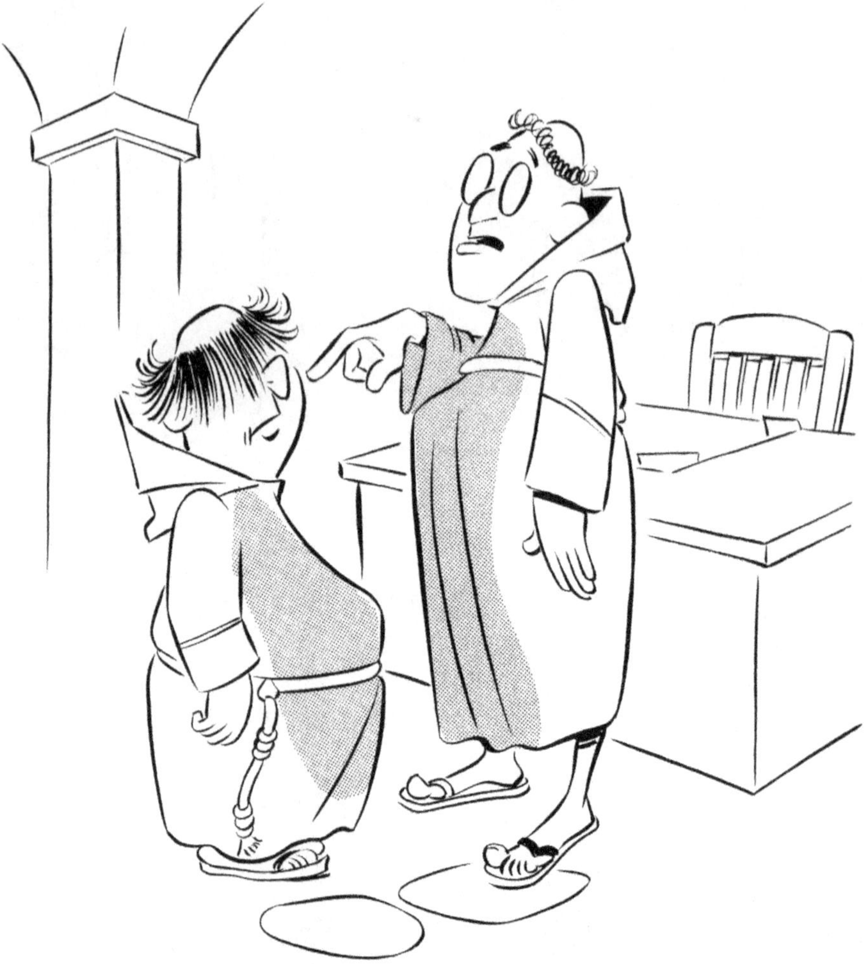

Well, stop feuding with the barber and get a haircut.

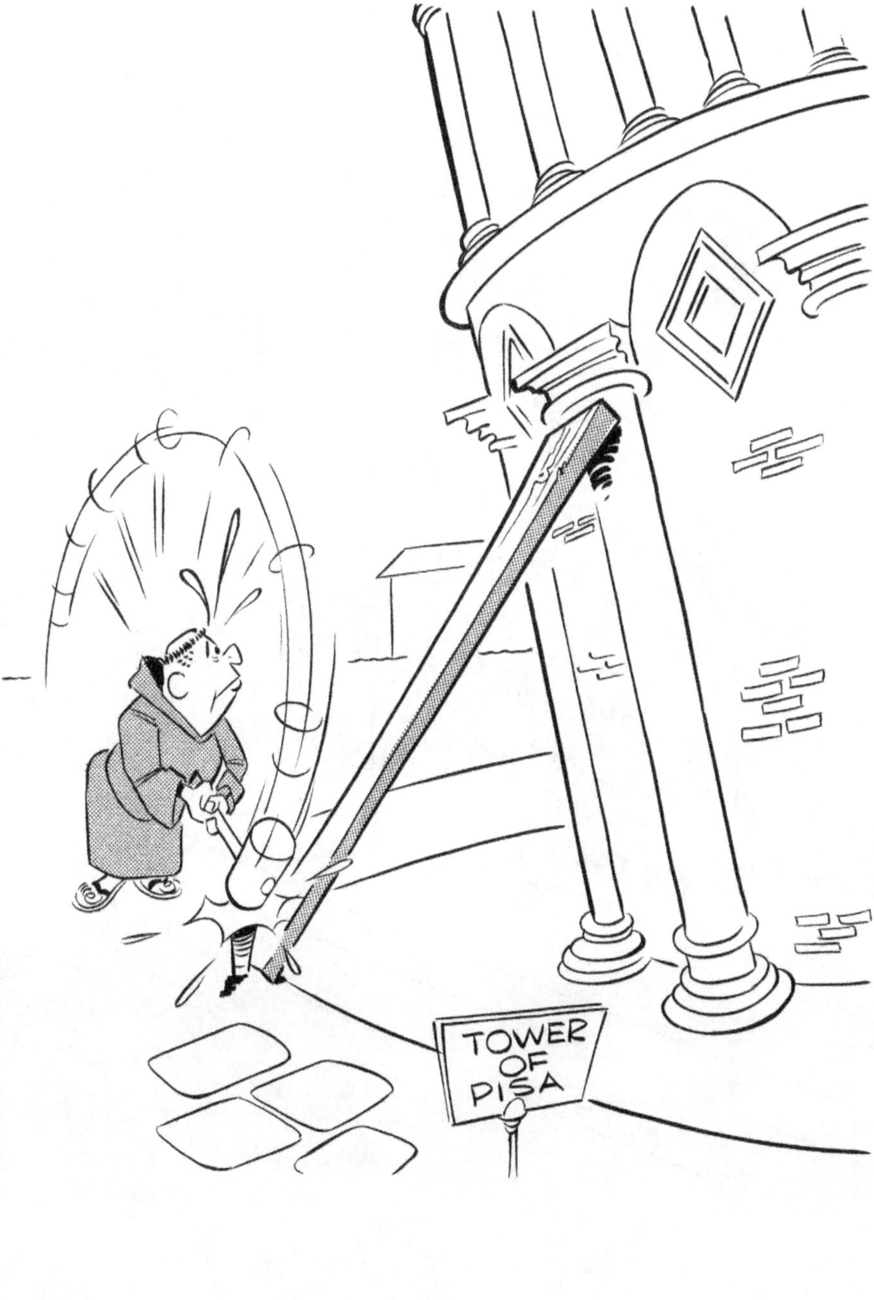
TOWER
OF
PISA

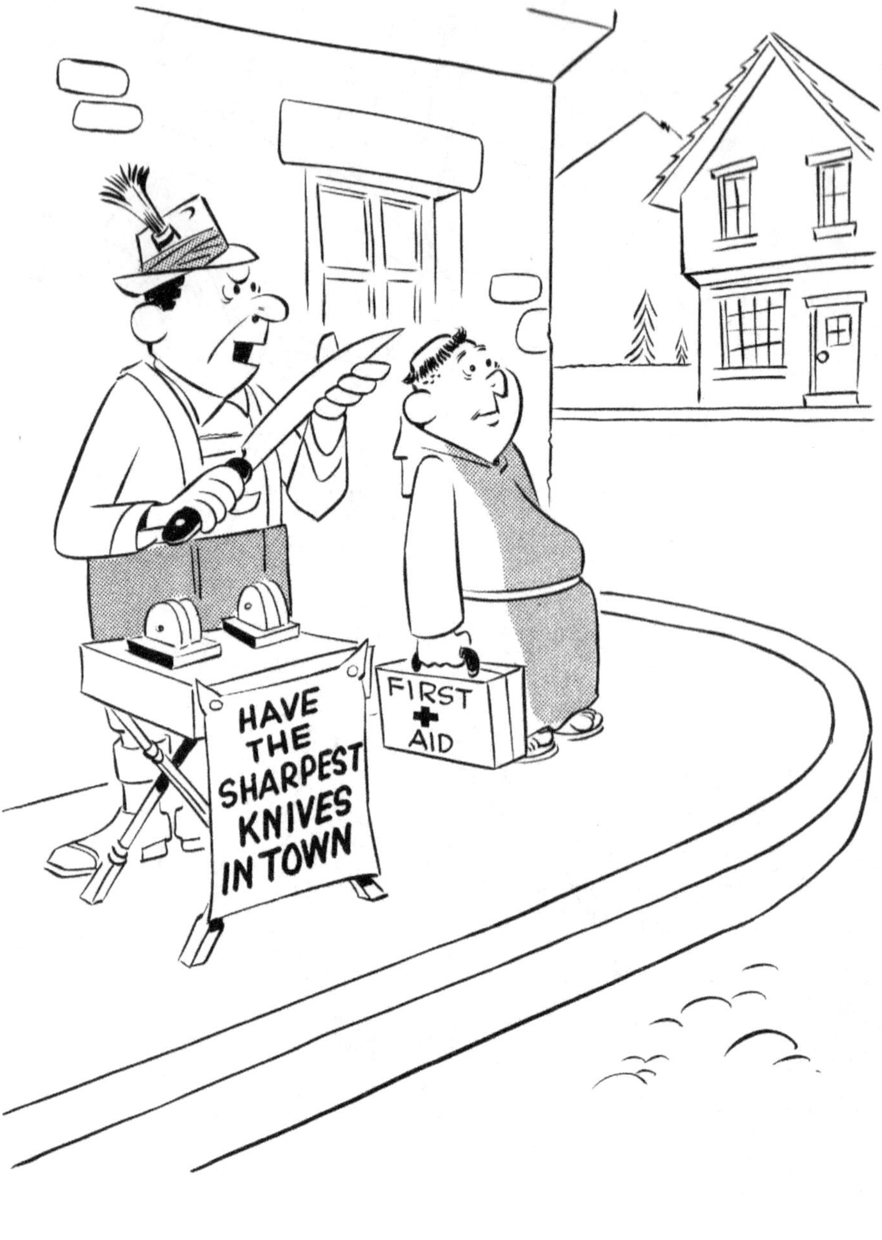
FIRST
AID
HAVE THE SHARPEST KNIVES IN TOWN

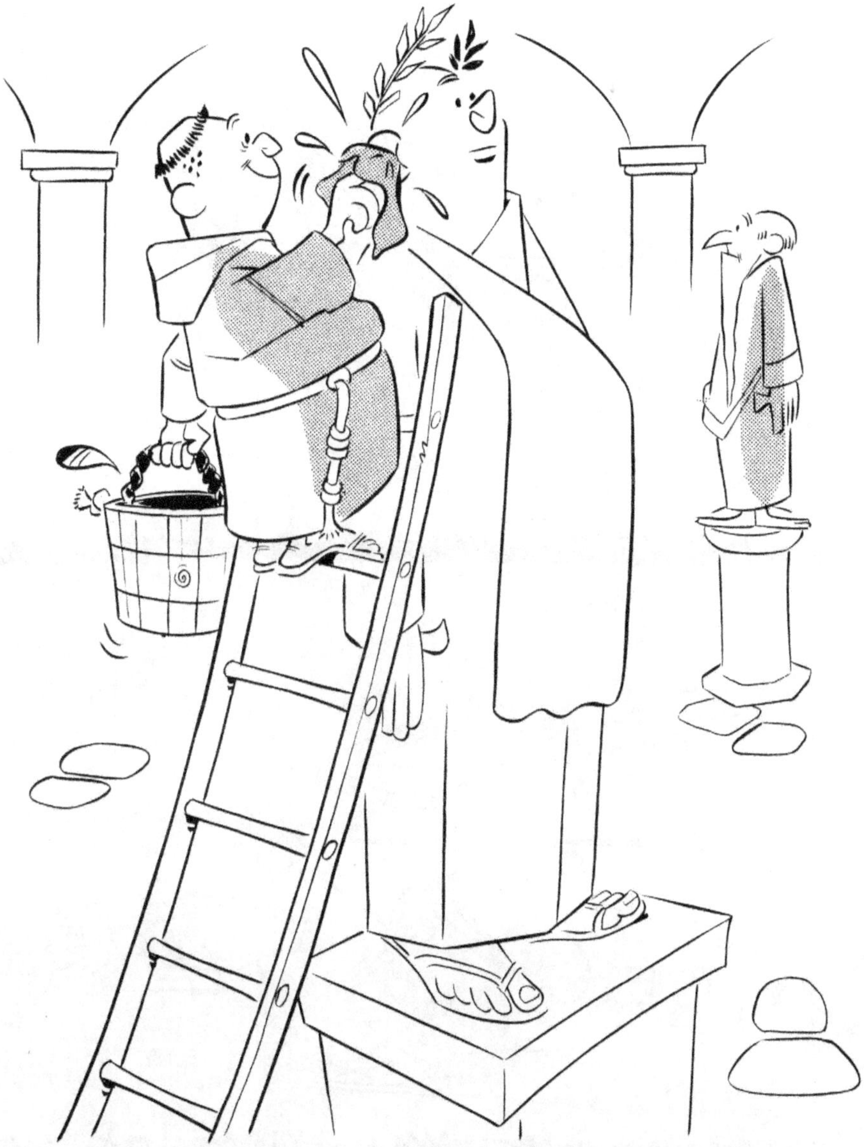

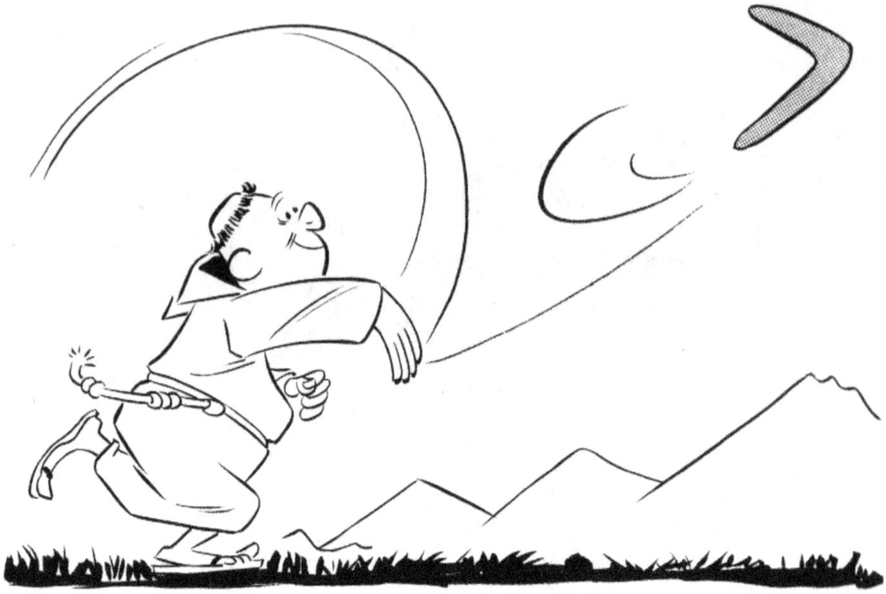

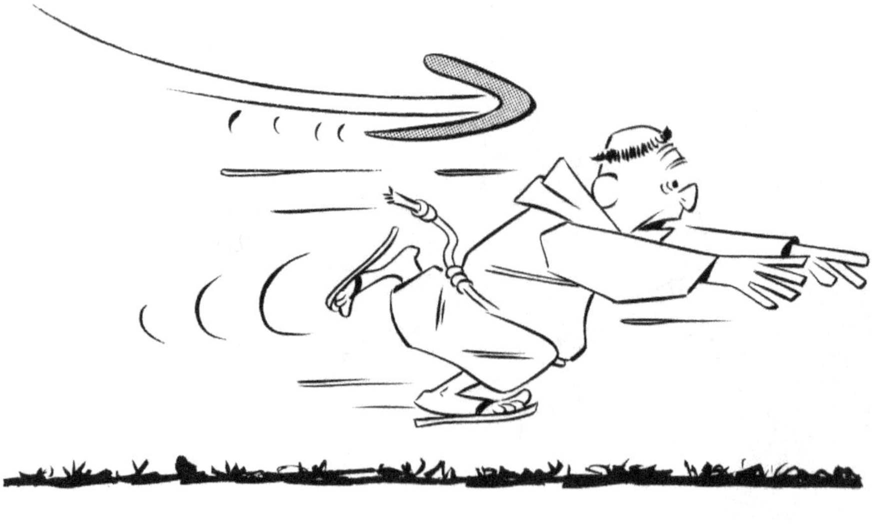

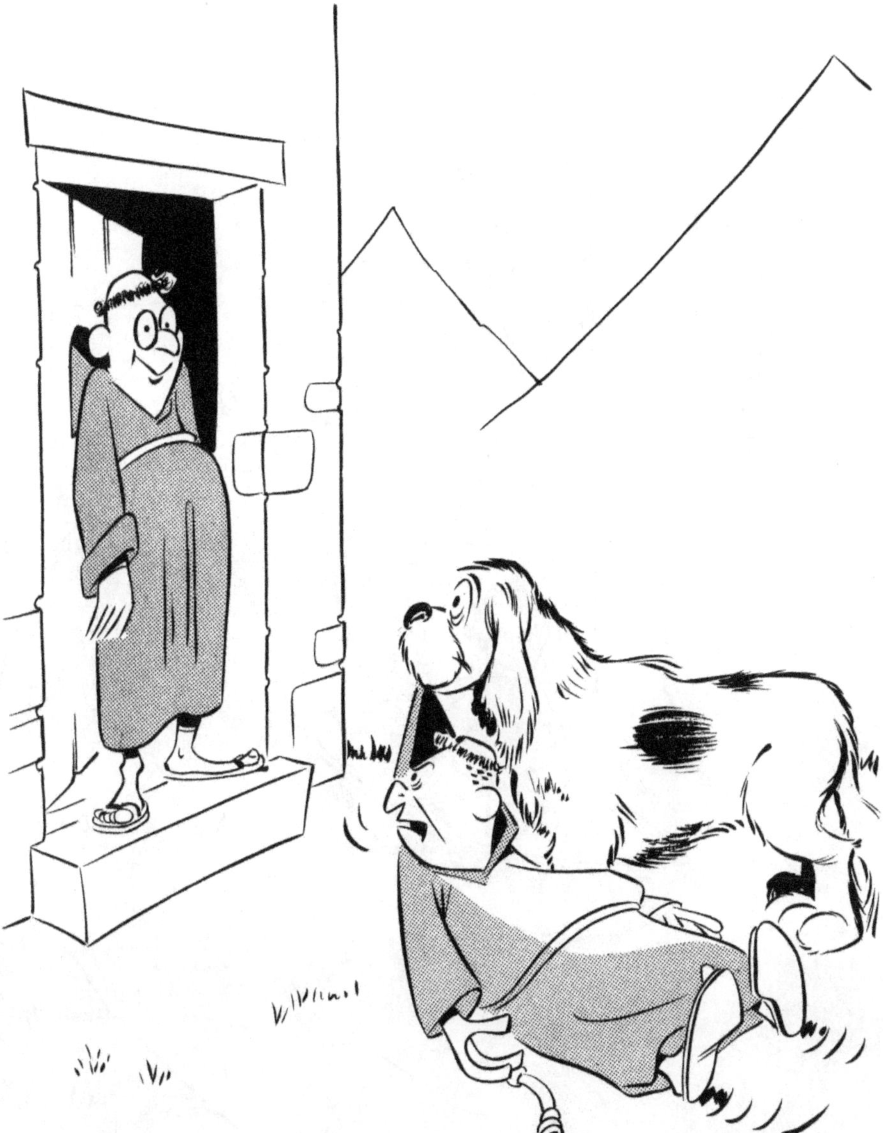

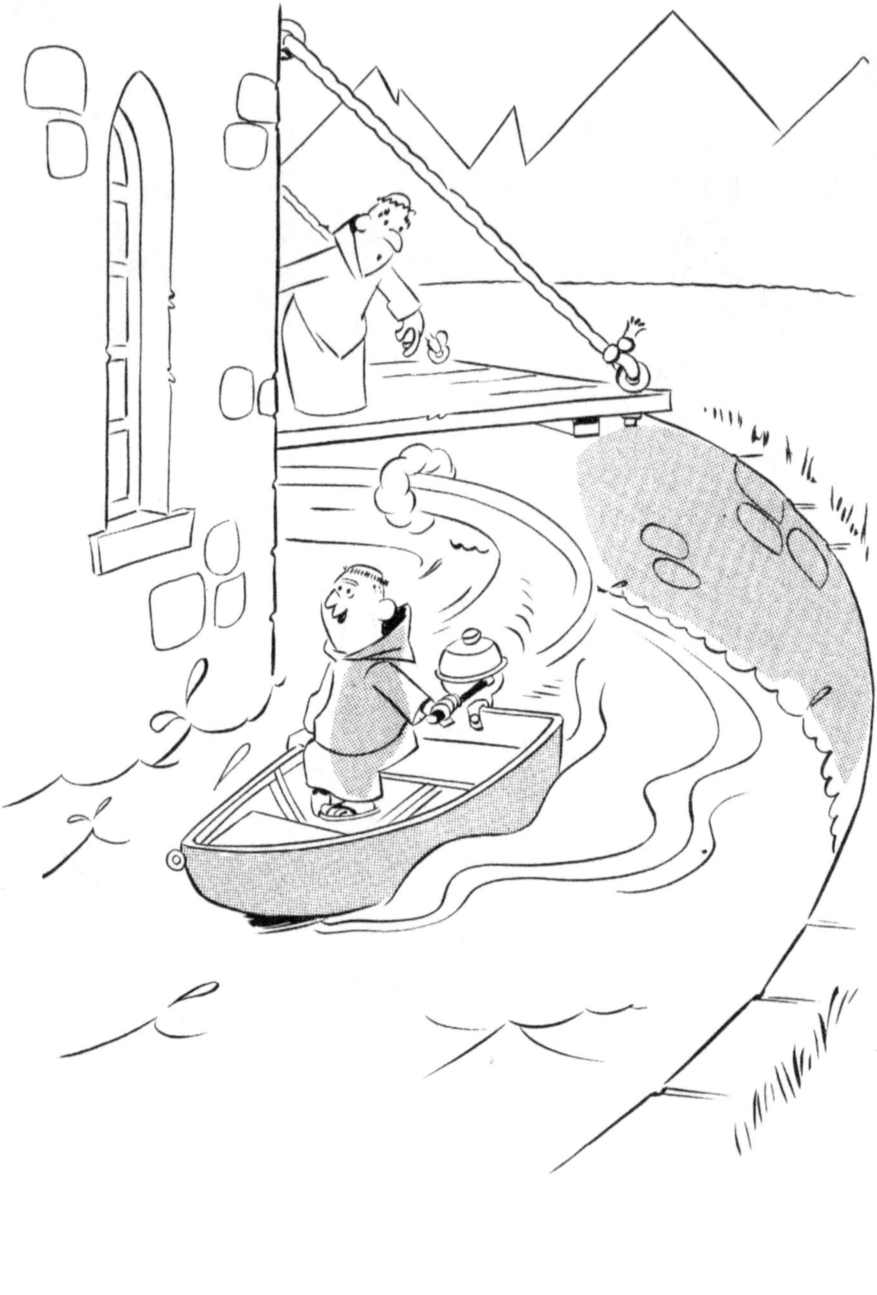

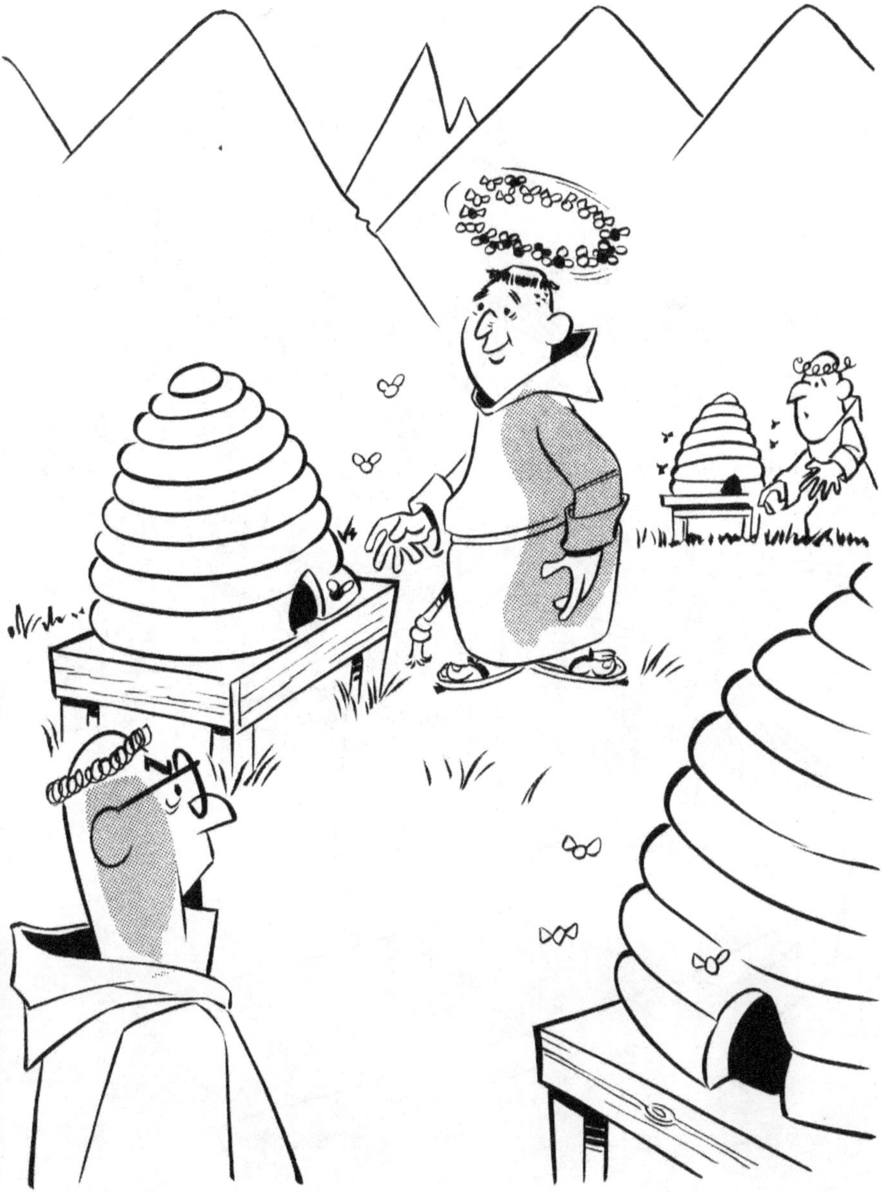

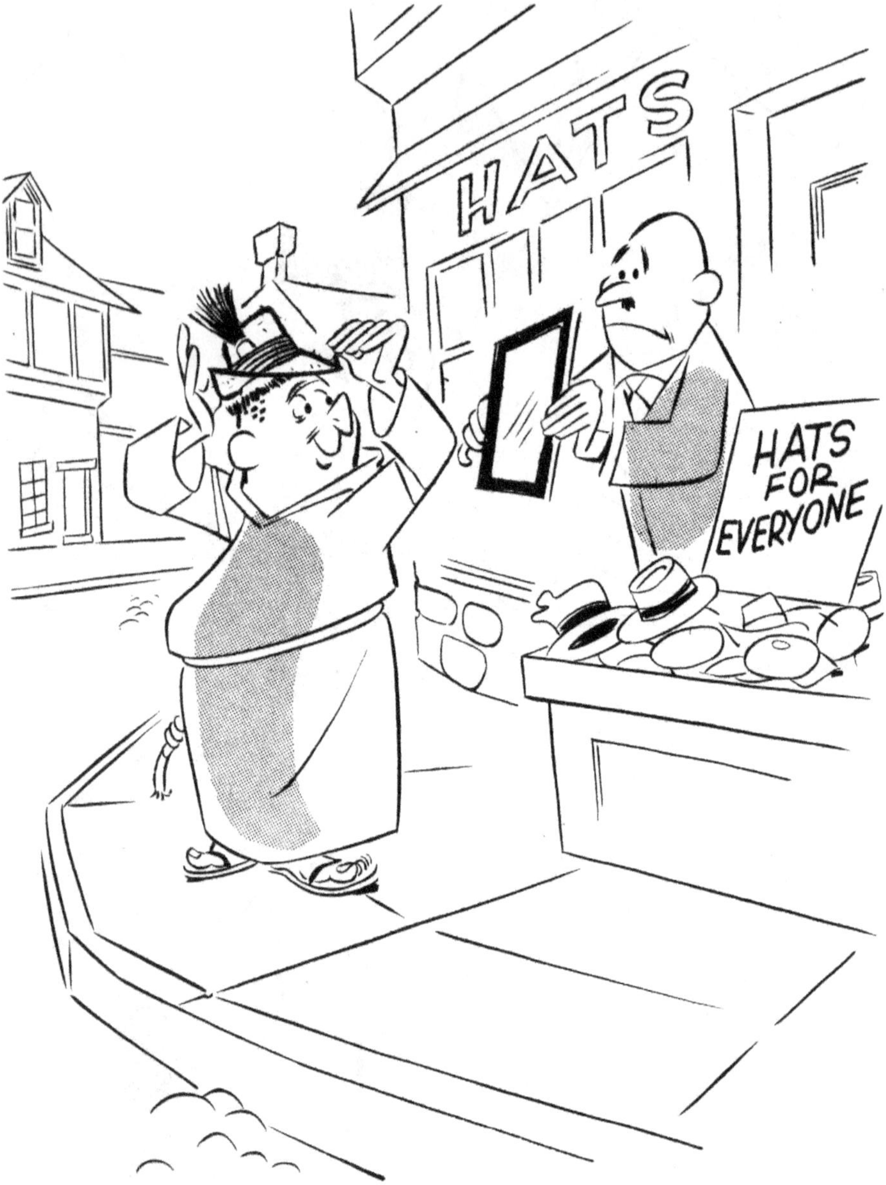

HATS
HATS FOR EVERYONE

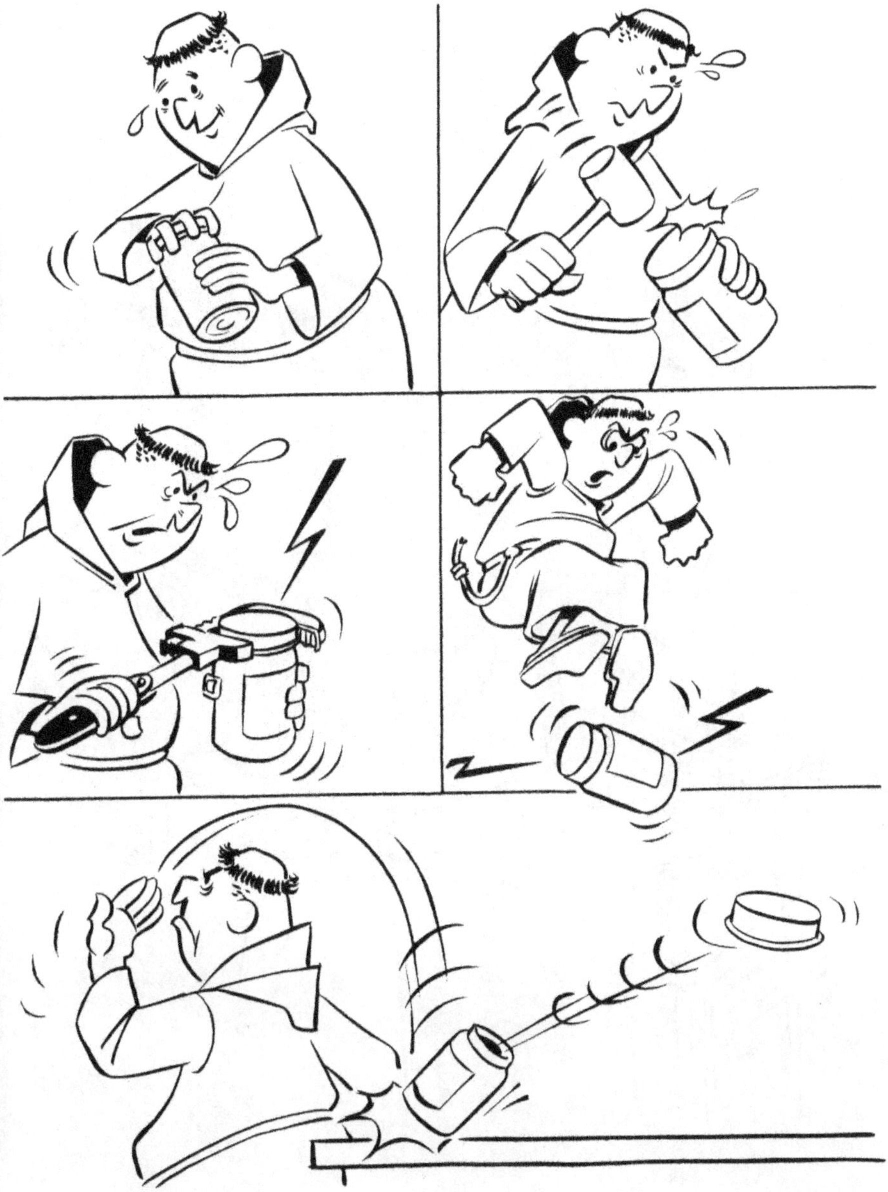

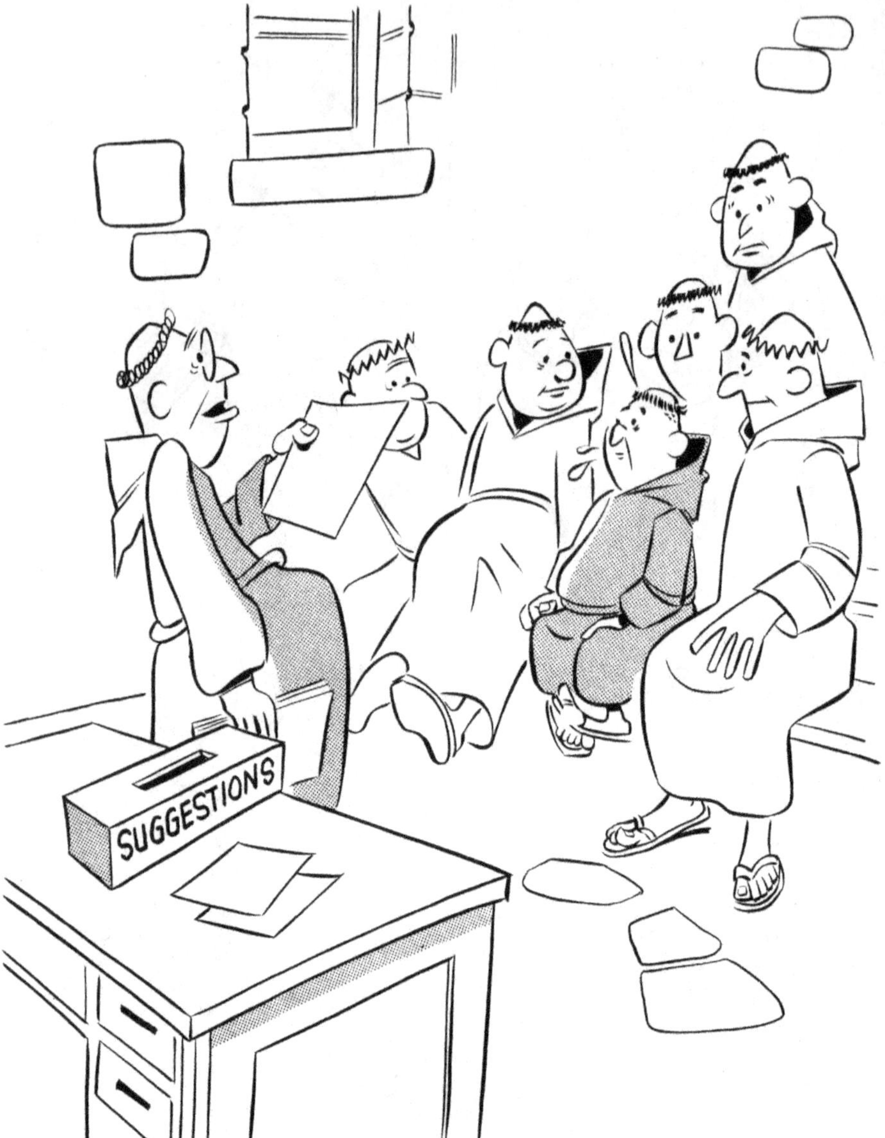
SUGGESTIONS

...And here is one signed "The Phantom".

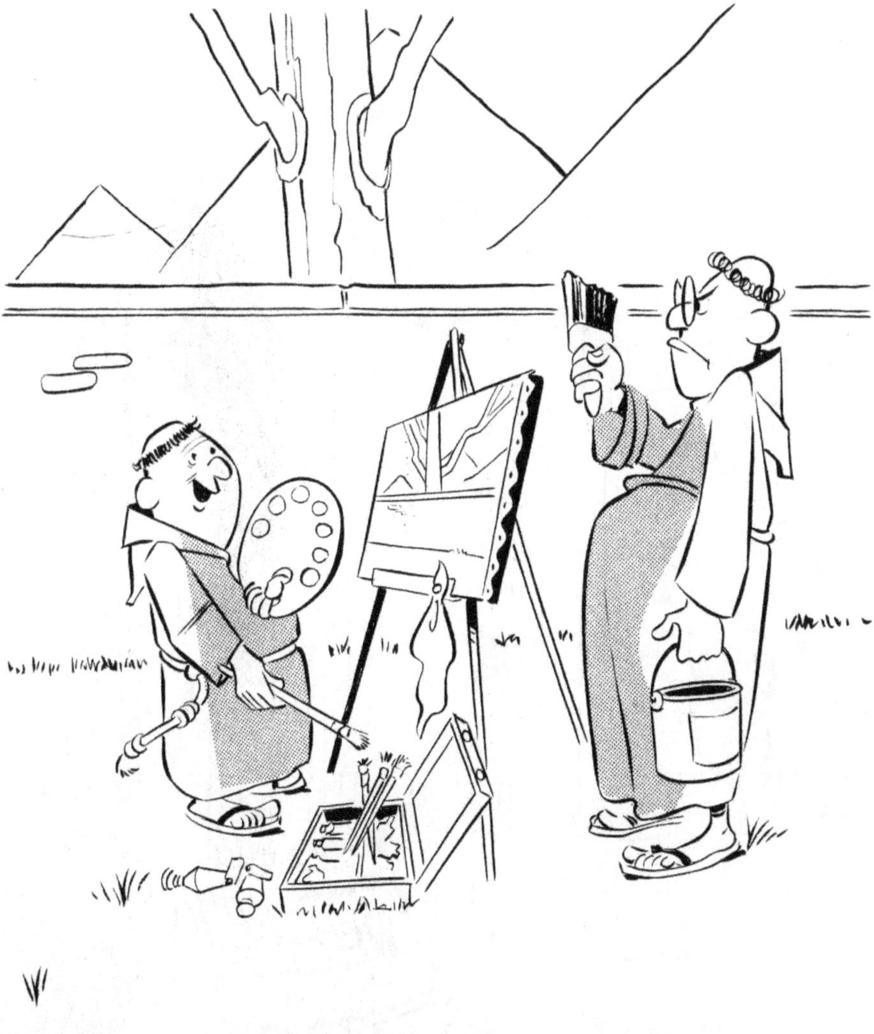

Didn't you say, "Paint the wall?"

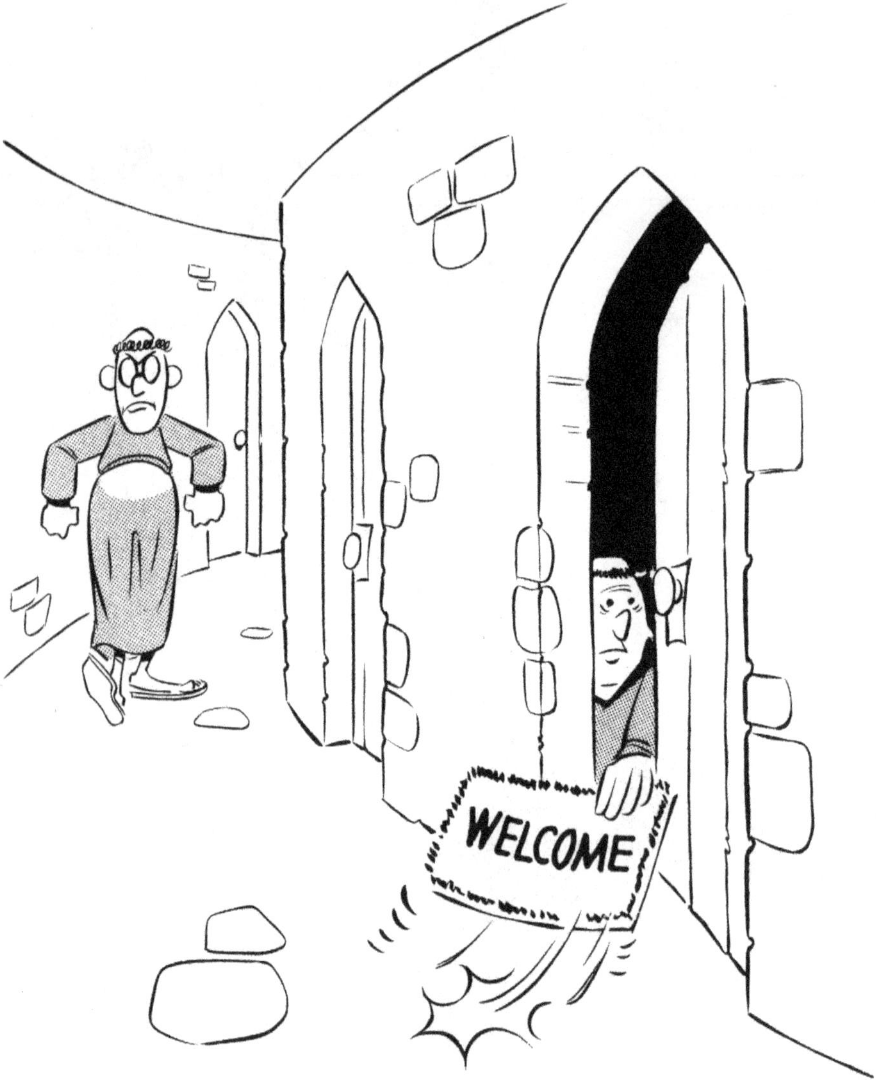
WELCOME

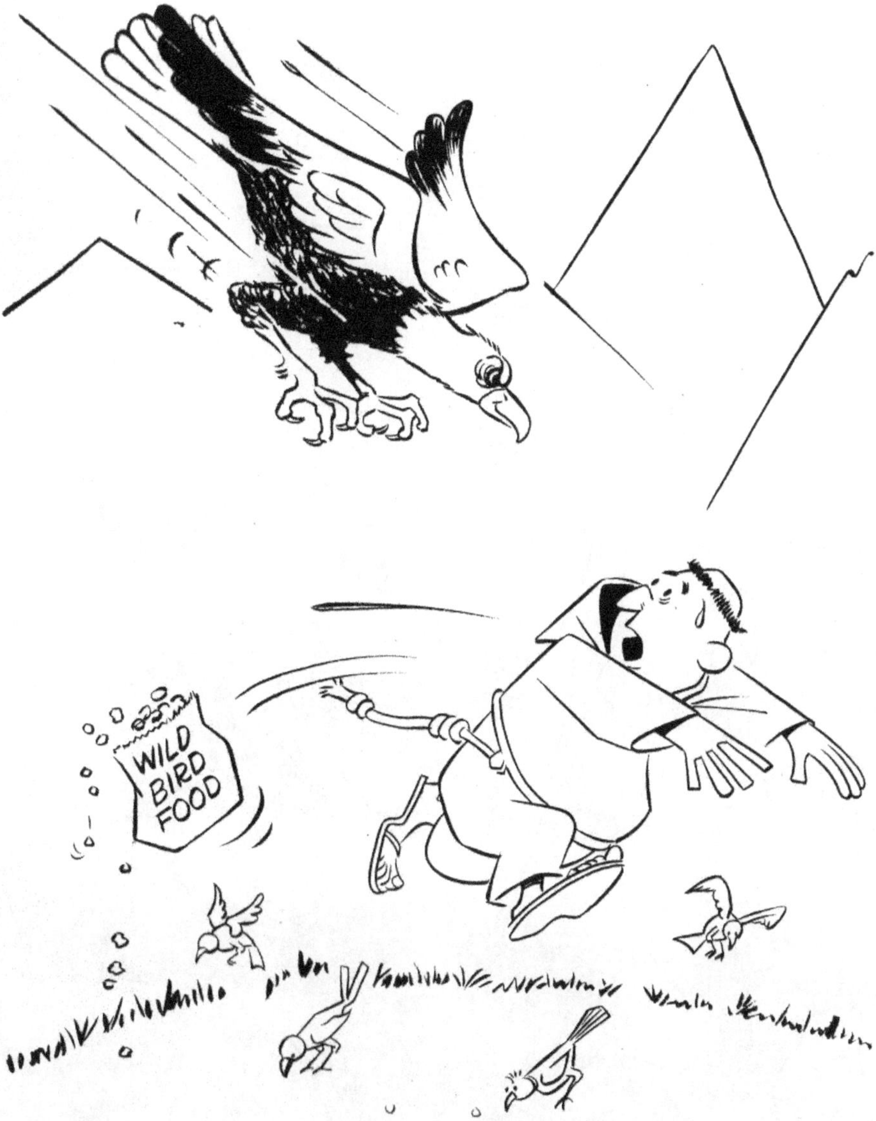
WILD
BIRD
FOOD

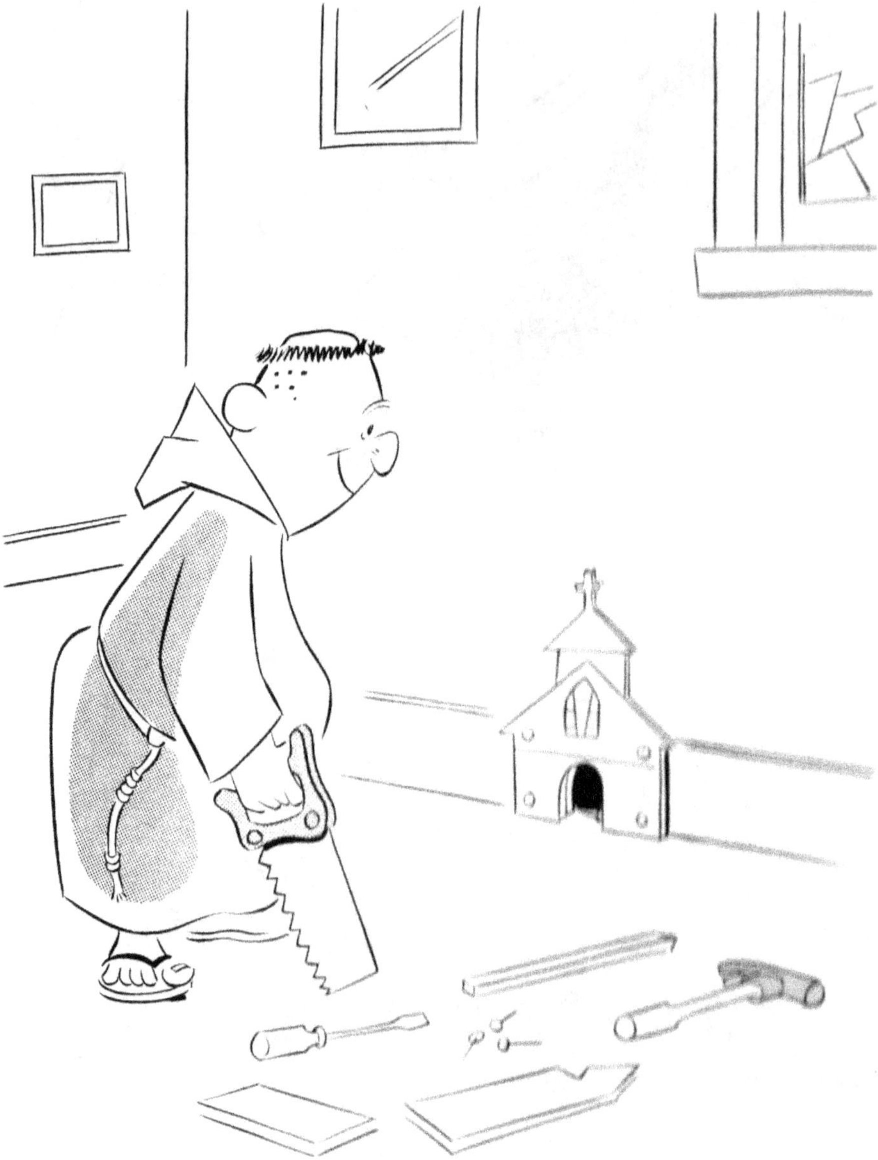

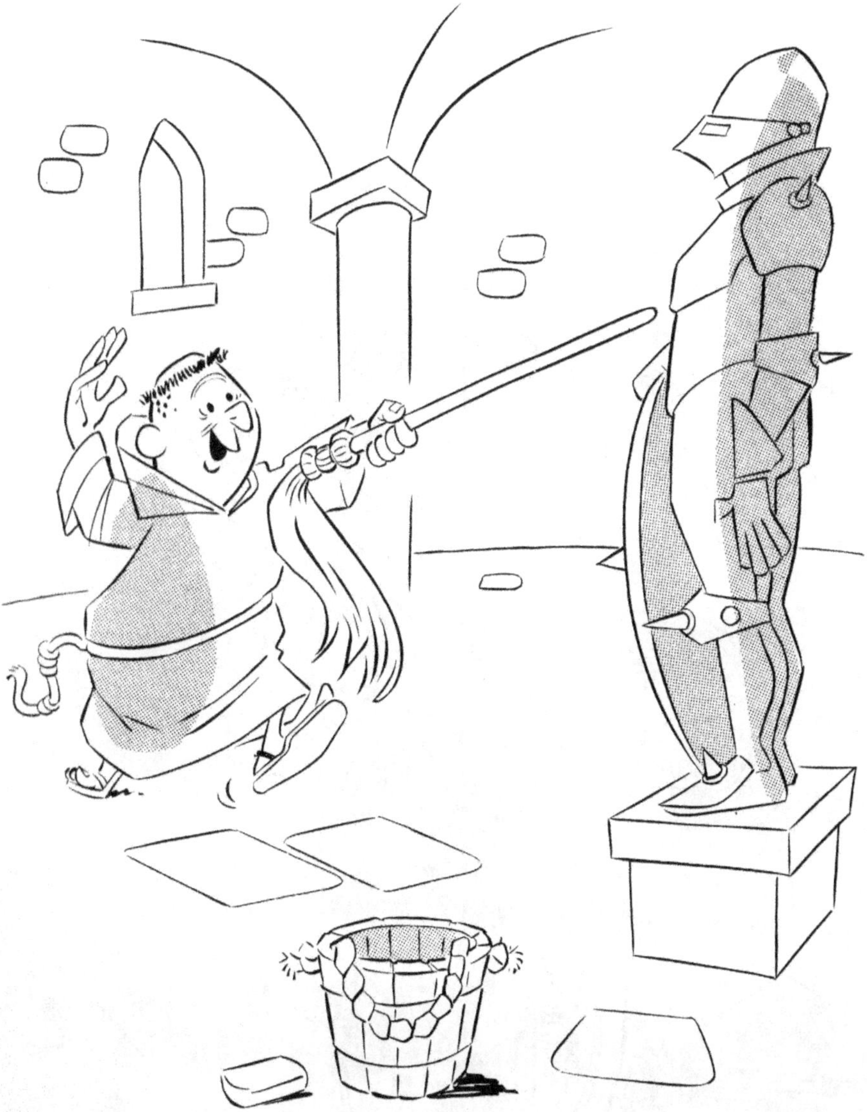

En garde!

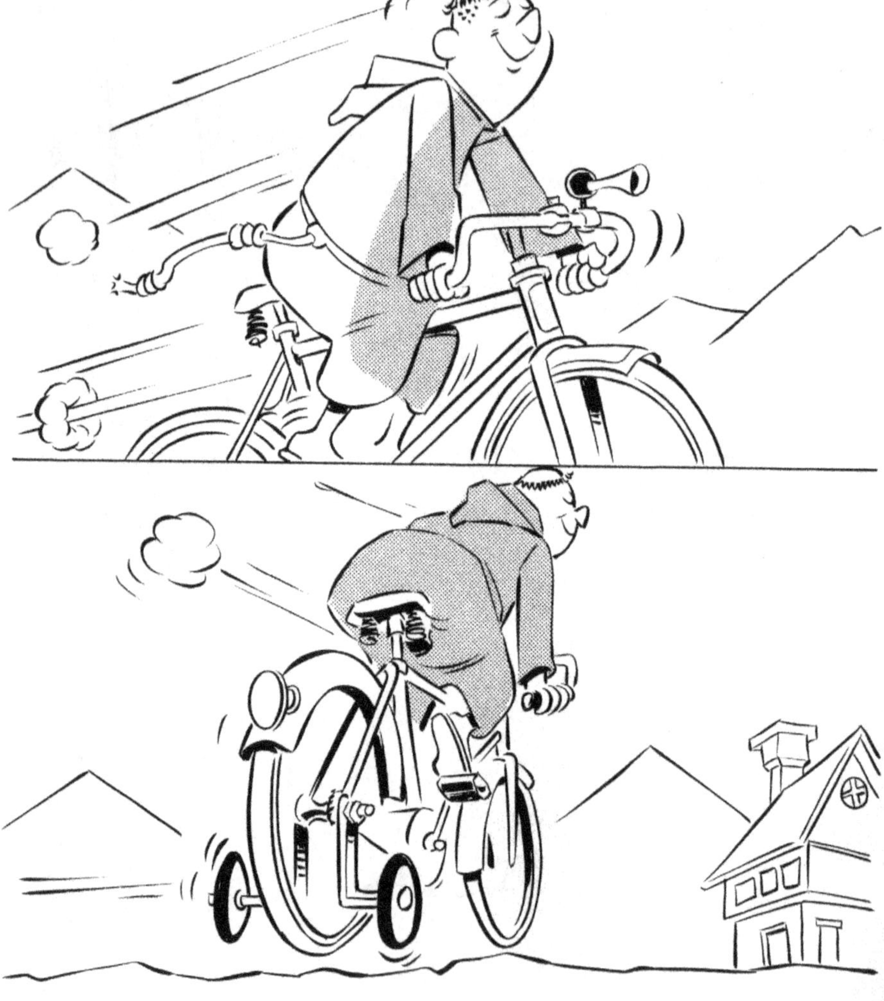

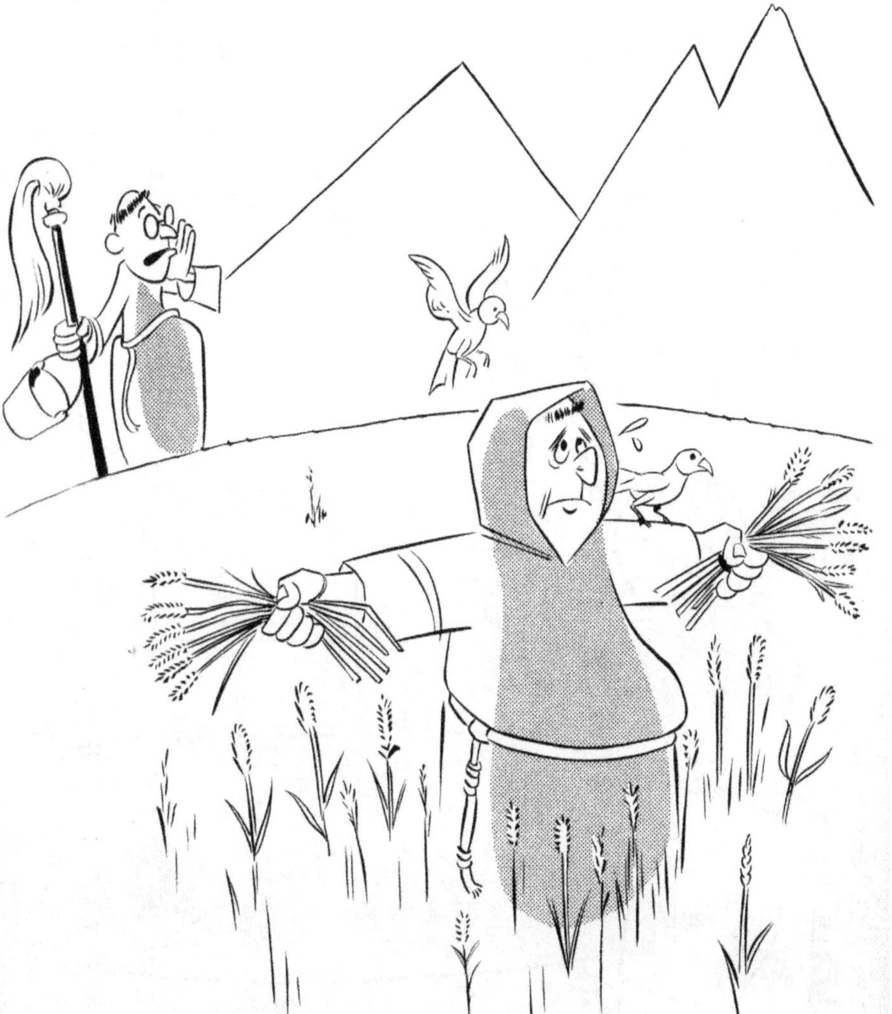

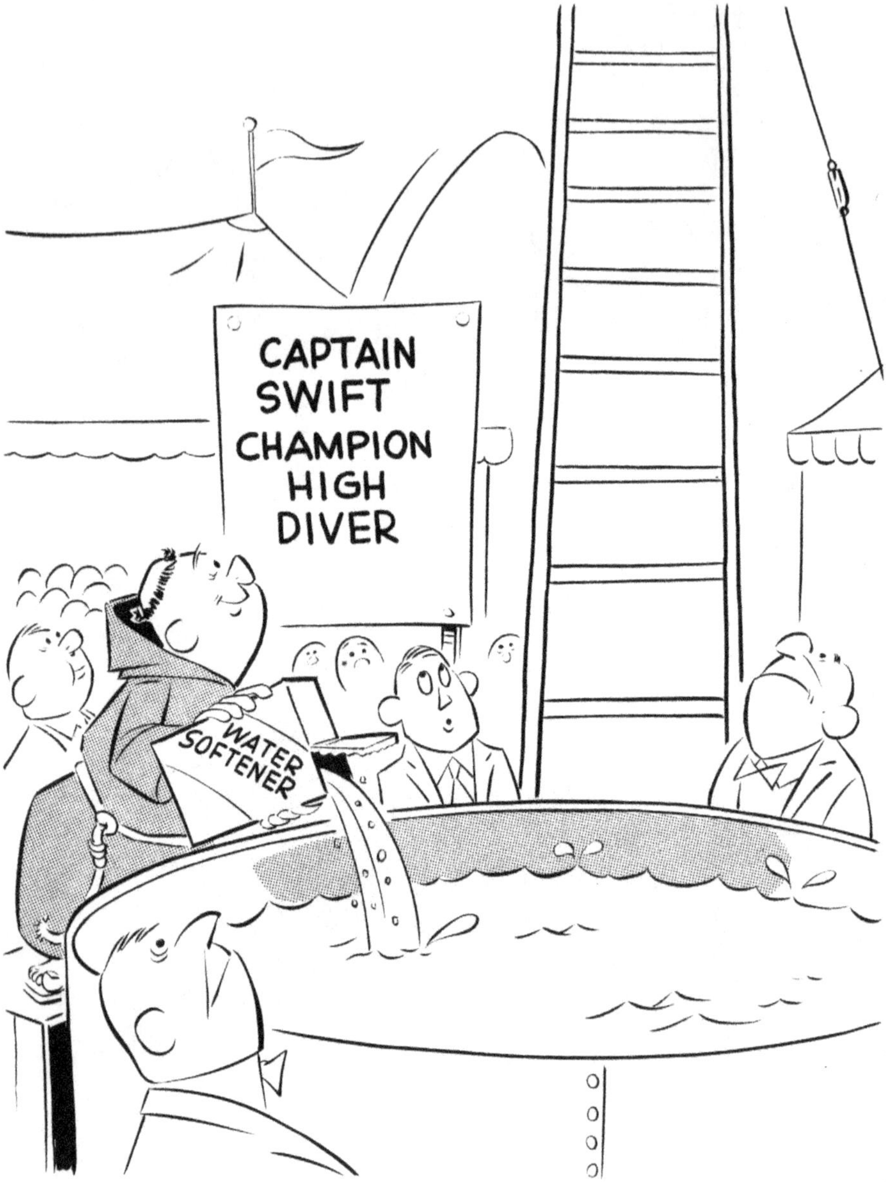
CAPTAIN SWIFT CHAMPION HIGH DIVER
WATER SOFTENER

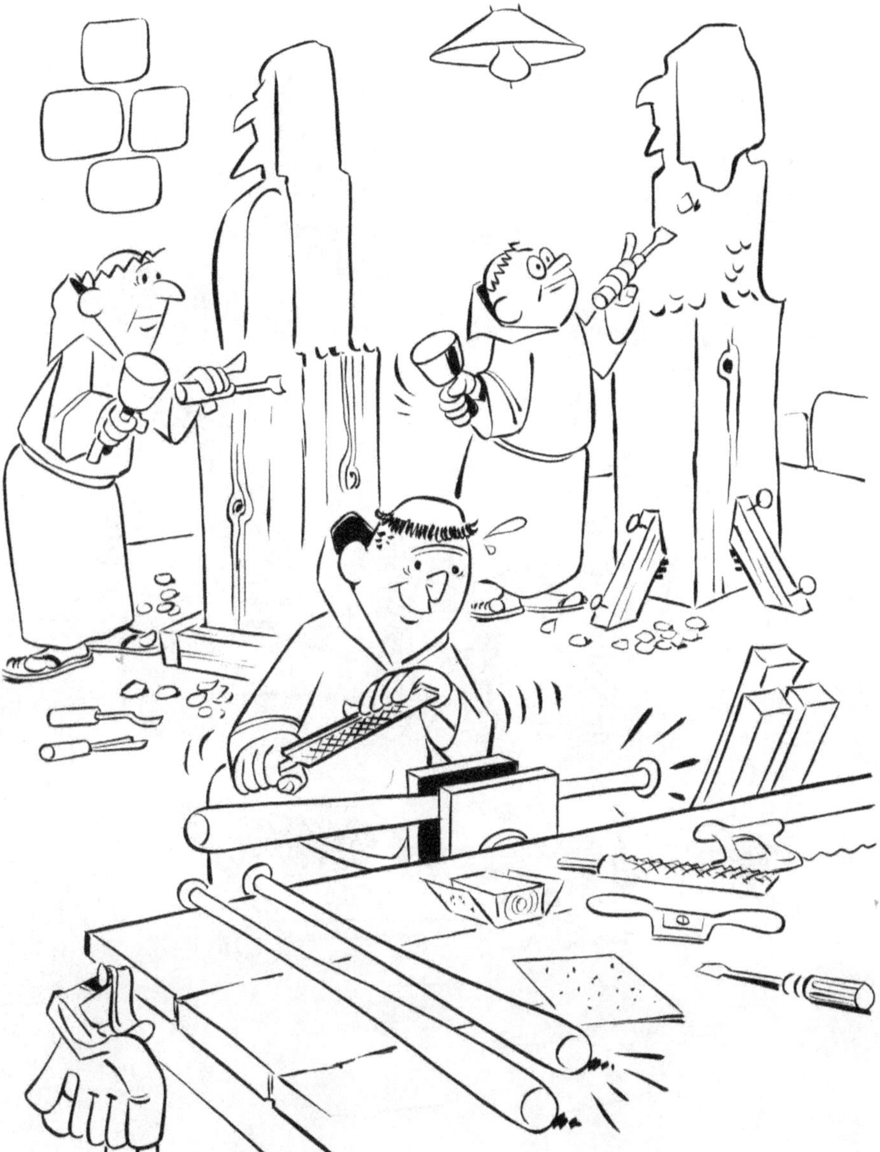

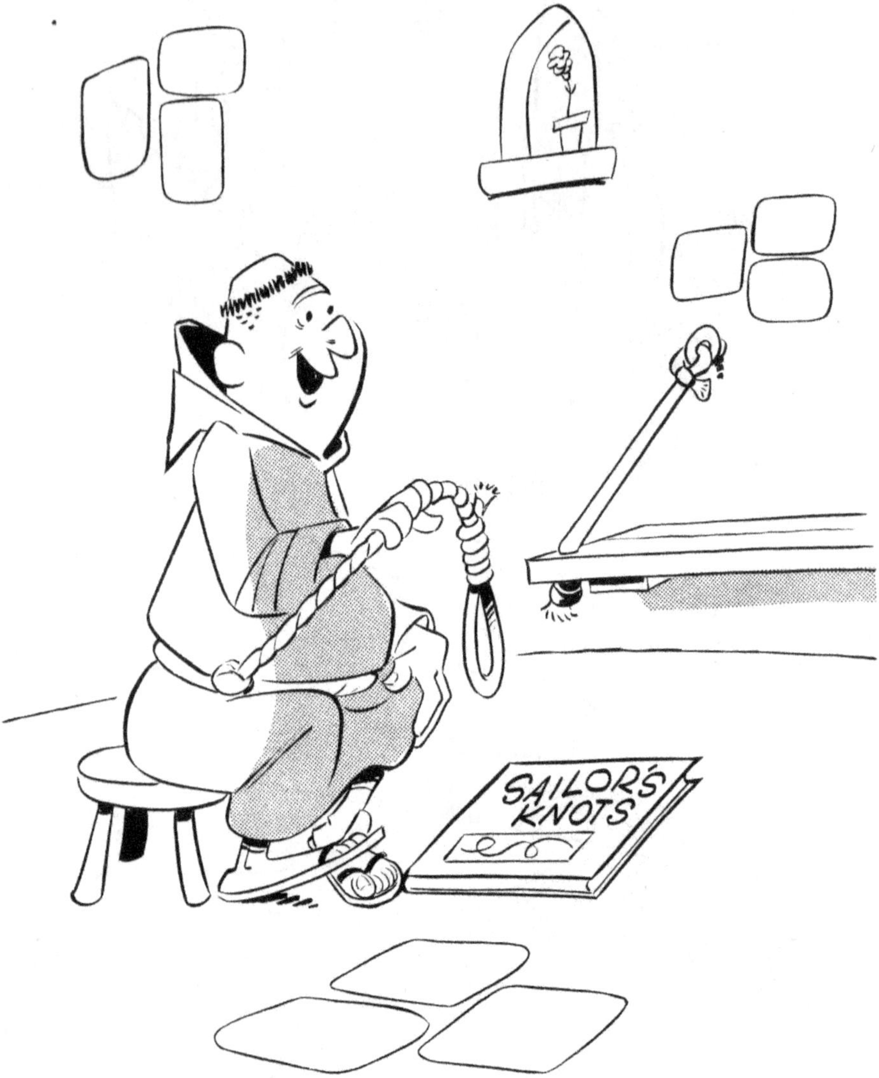
SAILOR'S
KNOTS

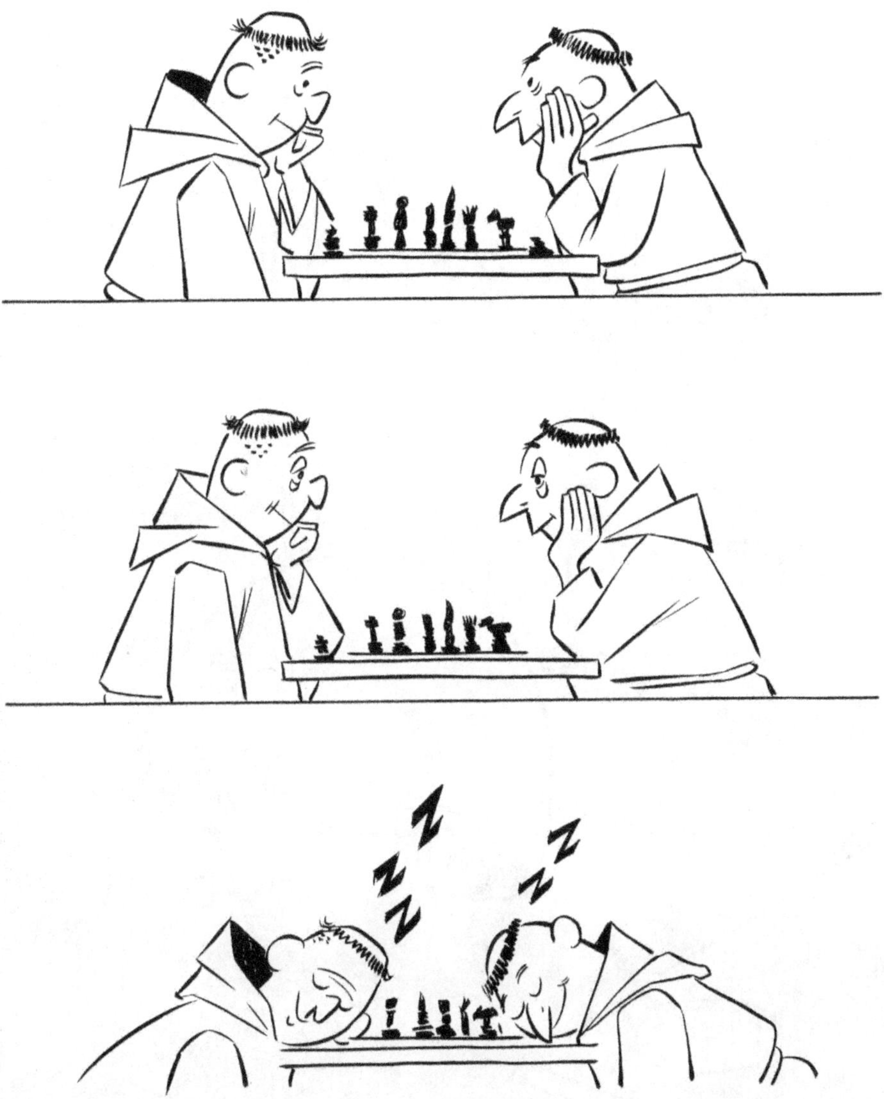

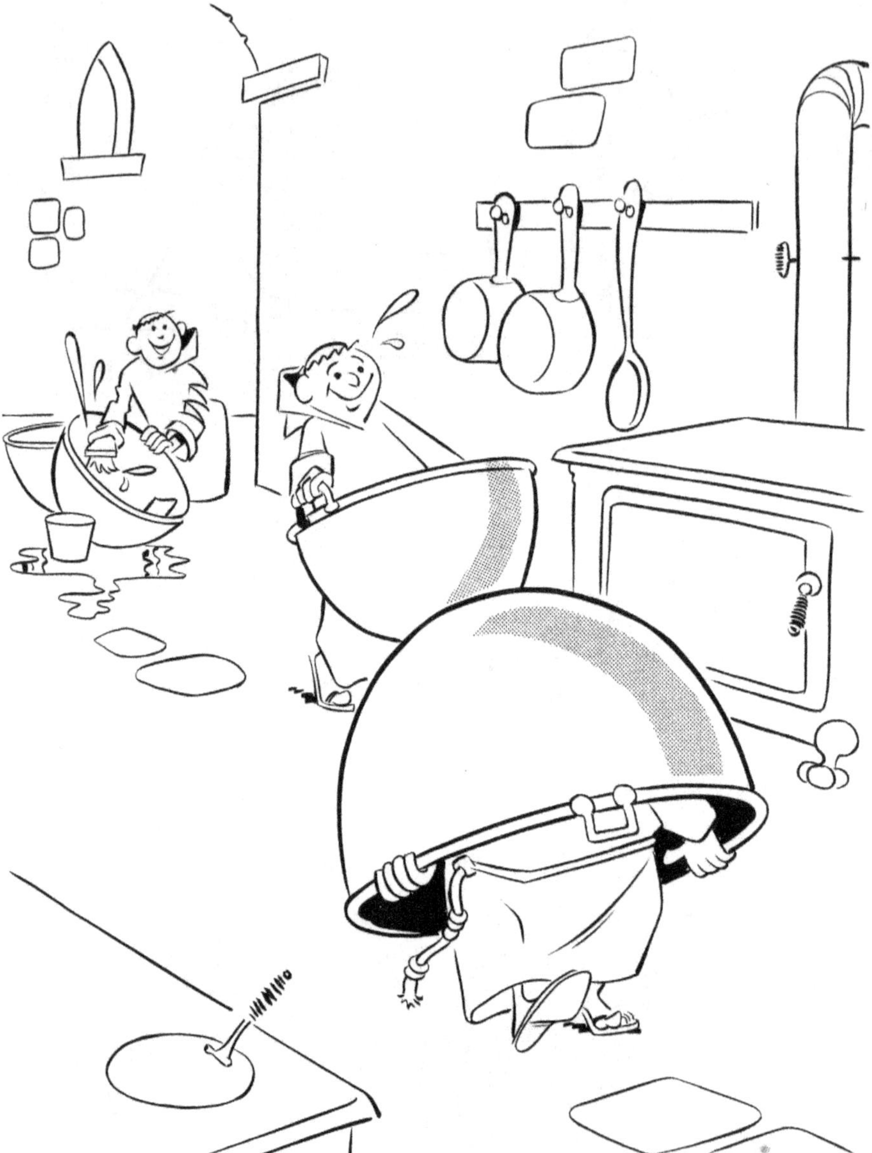

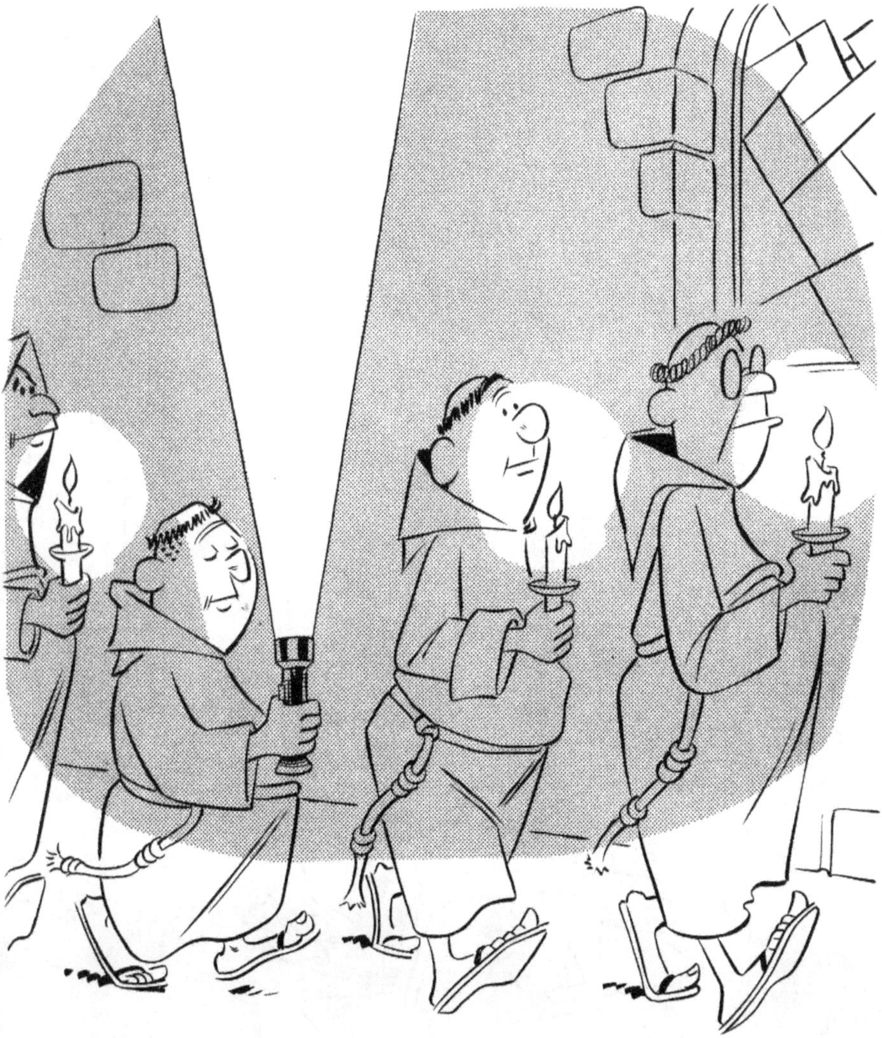

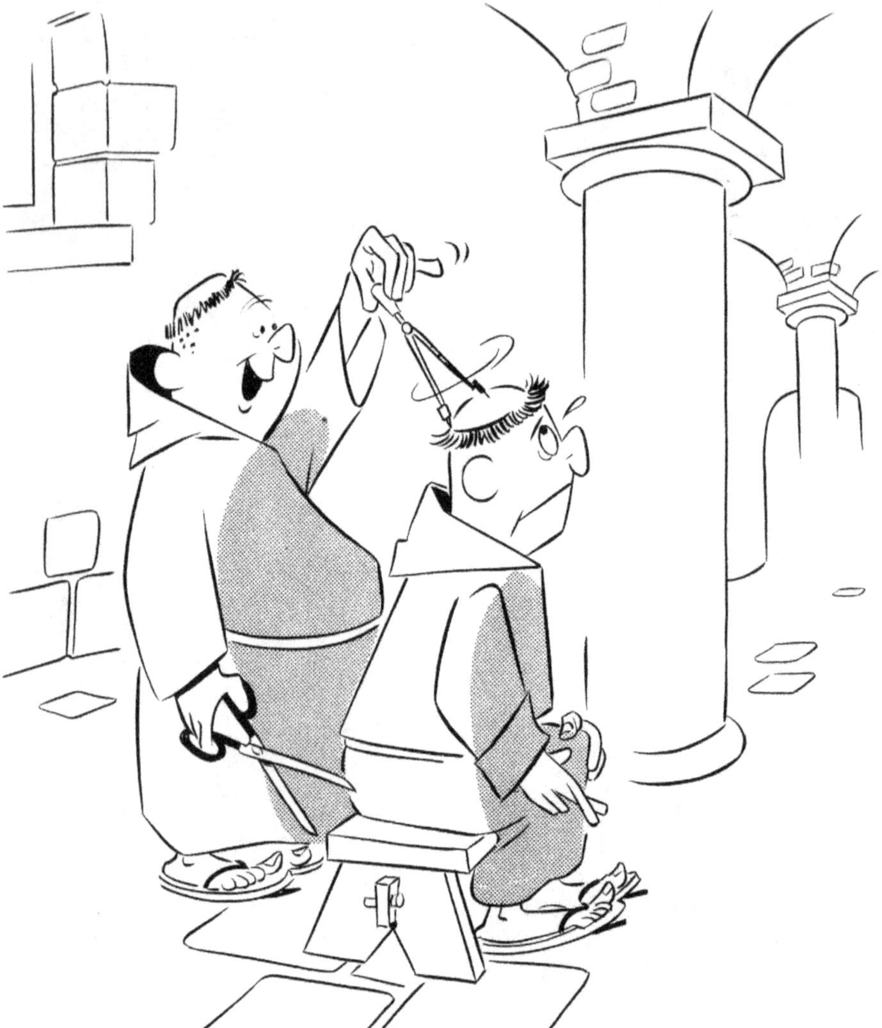

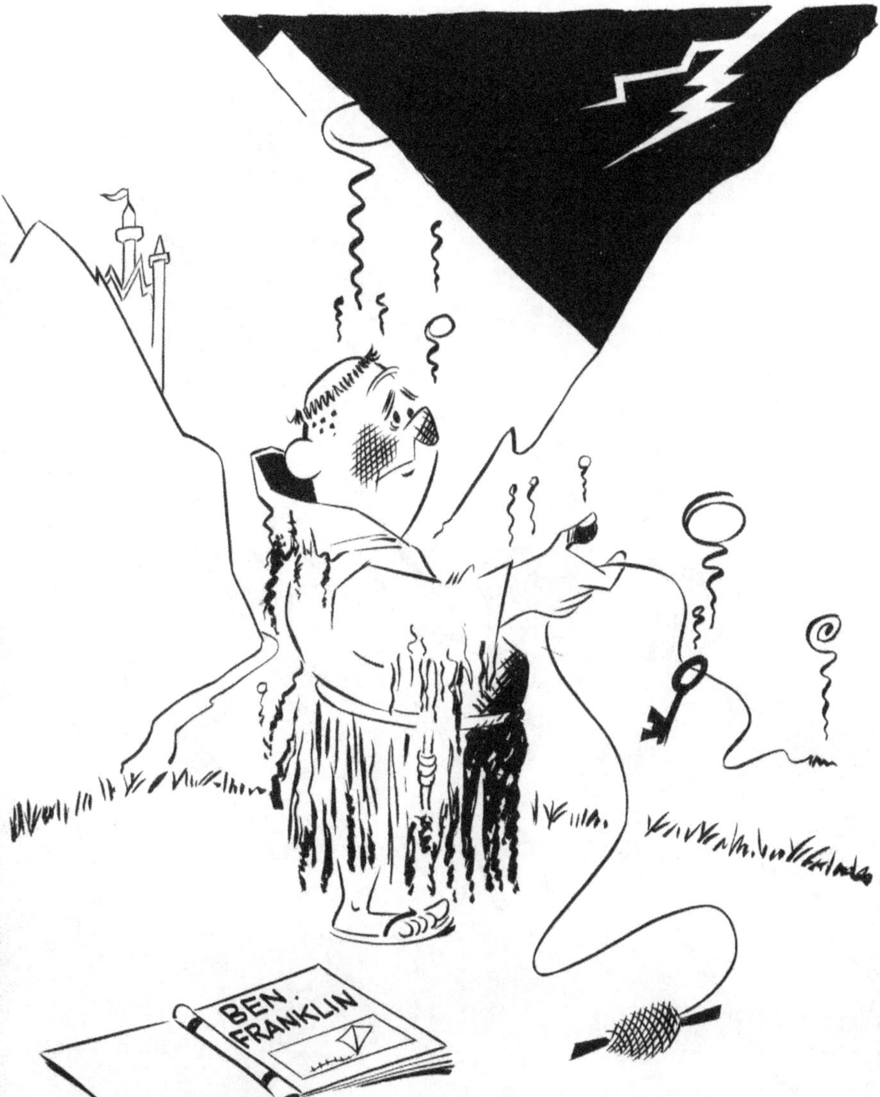
BEN. FRANKLIN

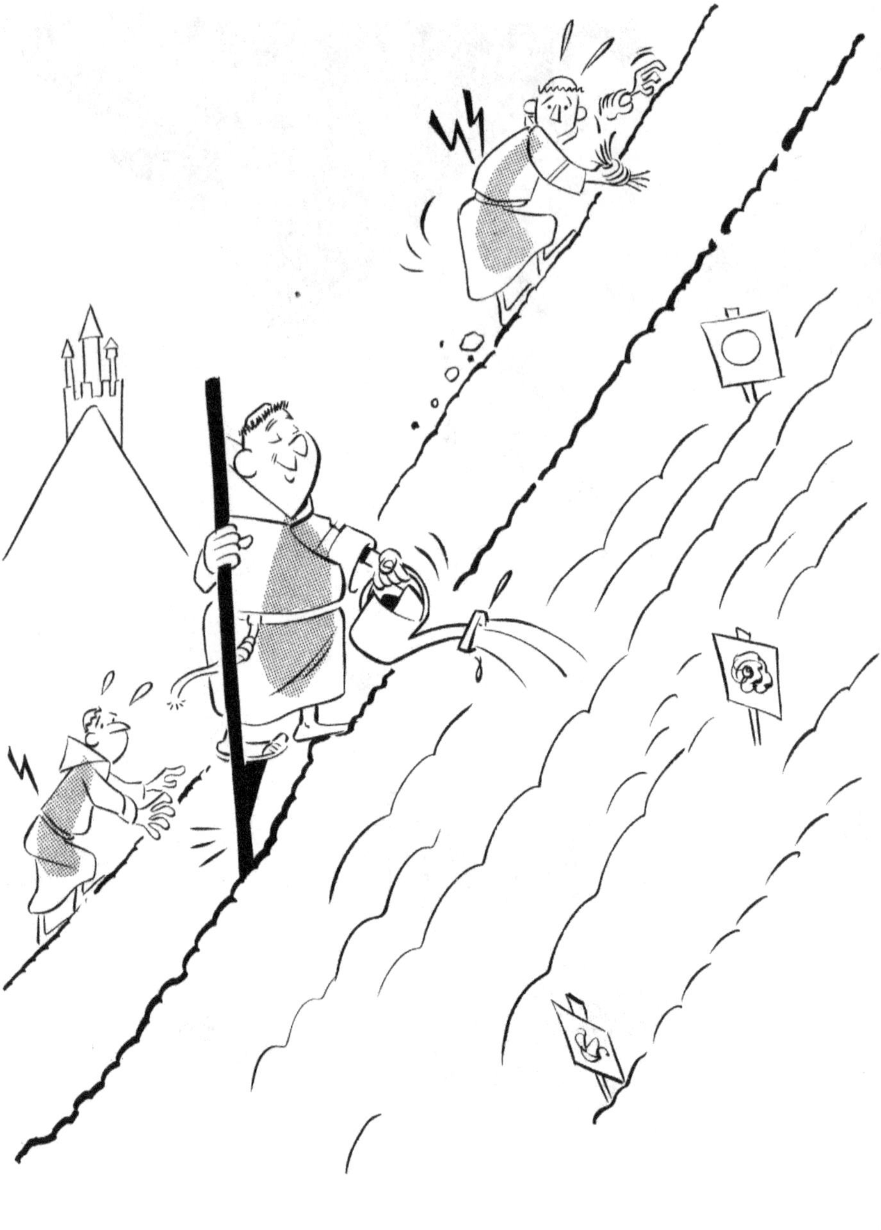

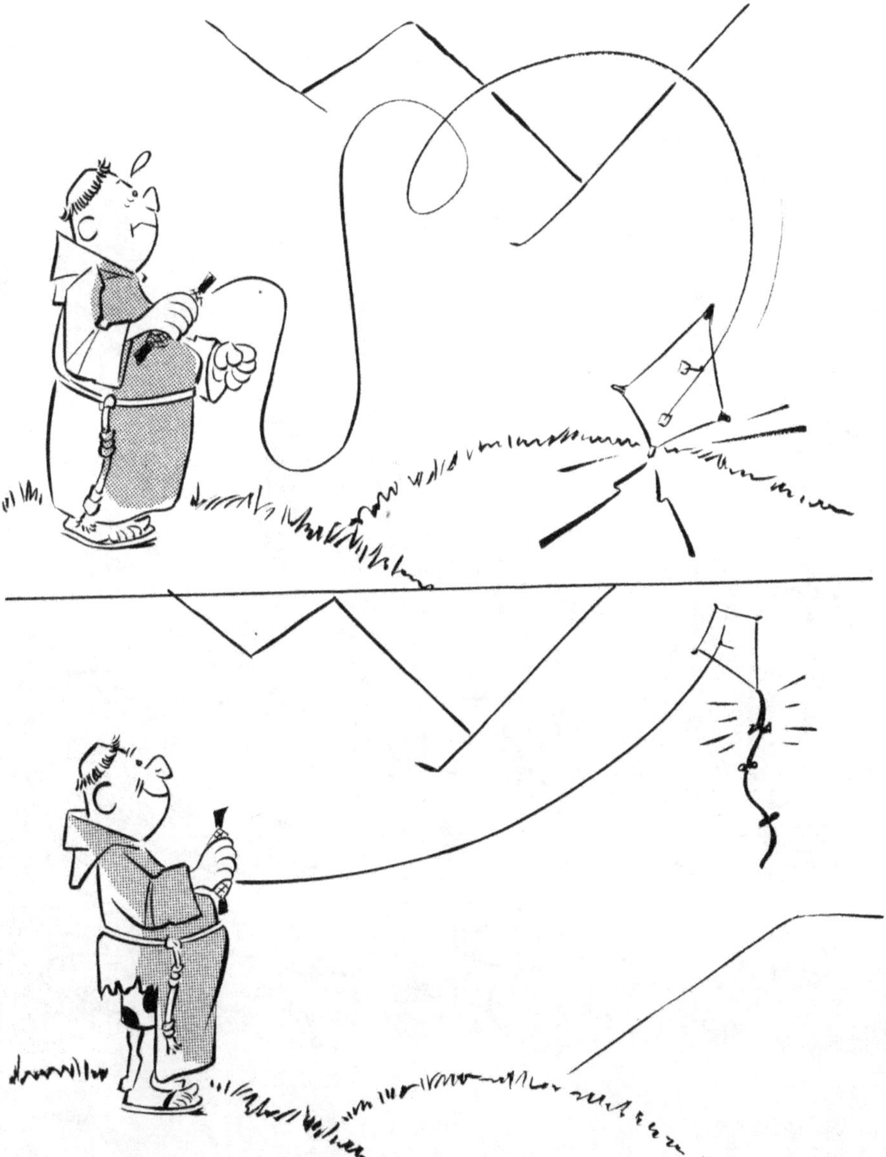

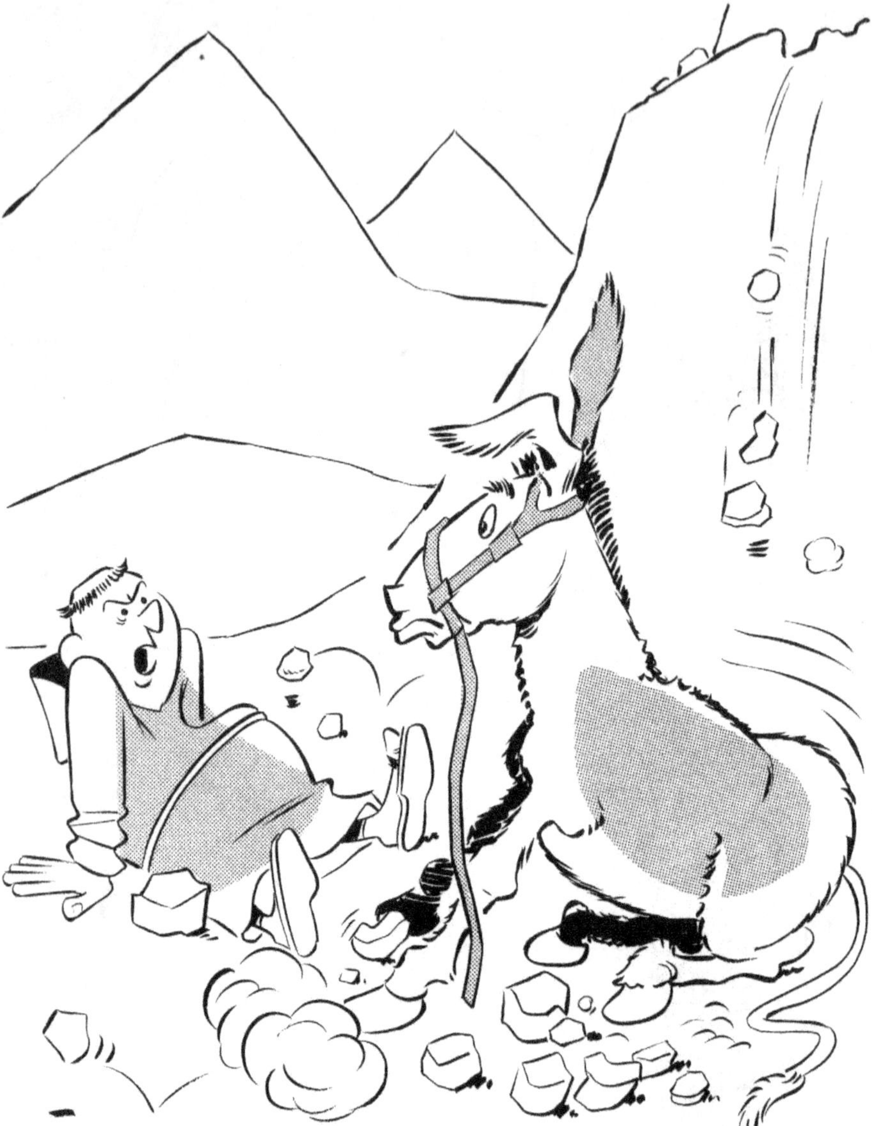

Sure-footed, my eye!

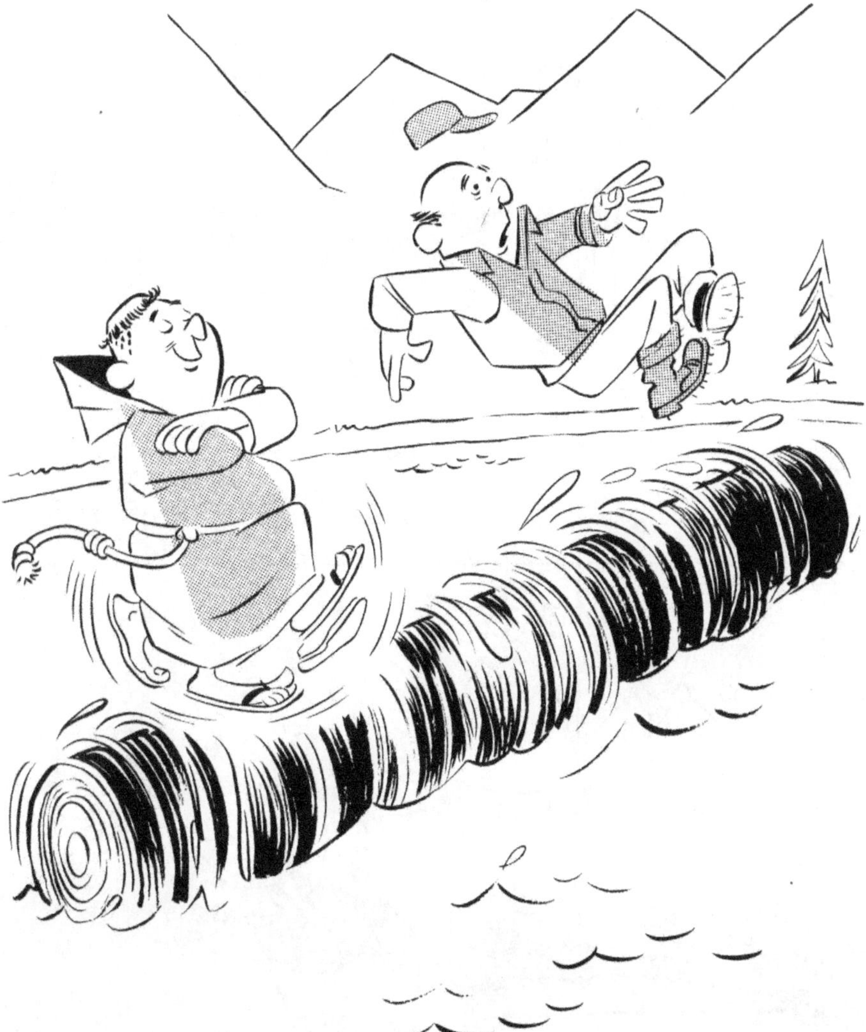

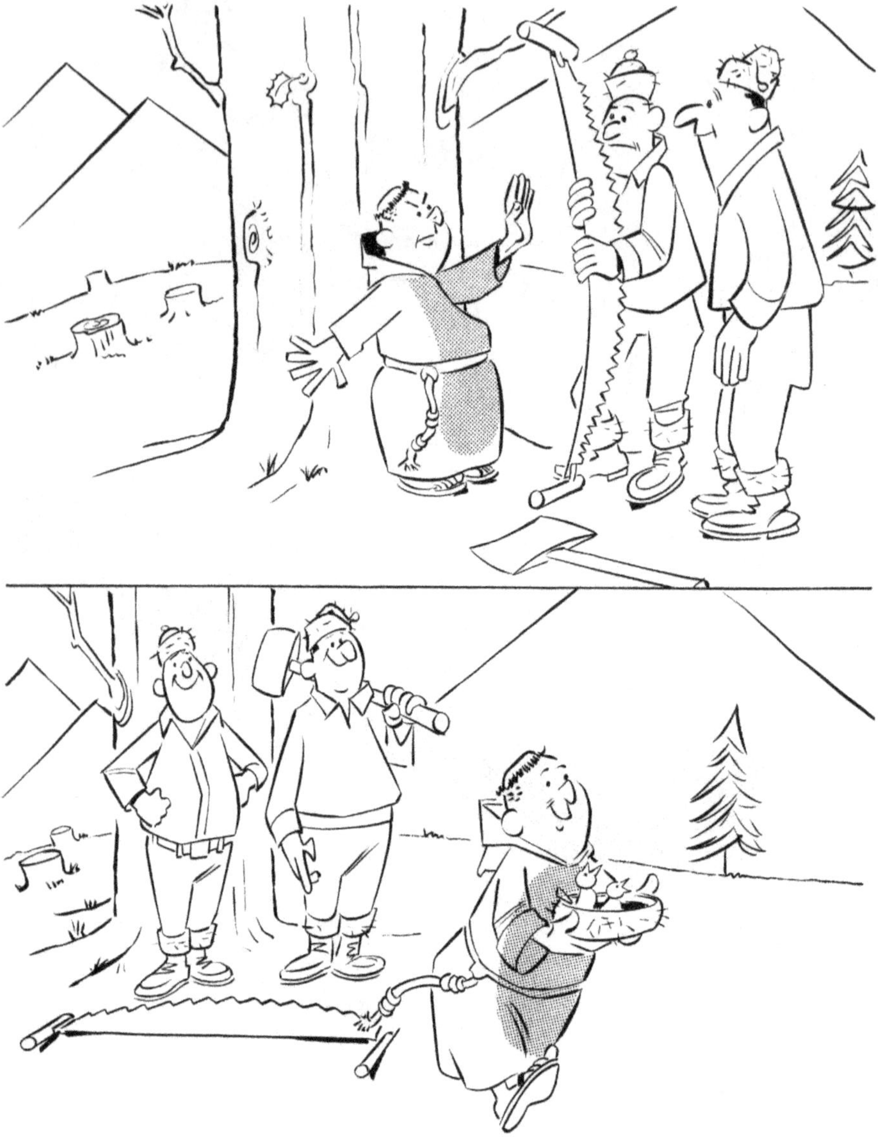

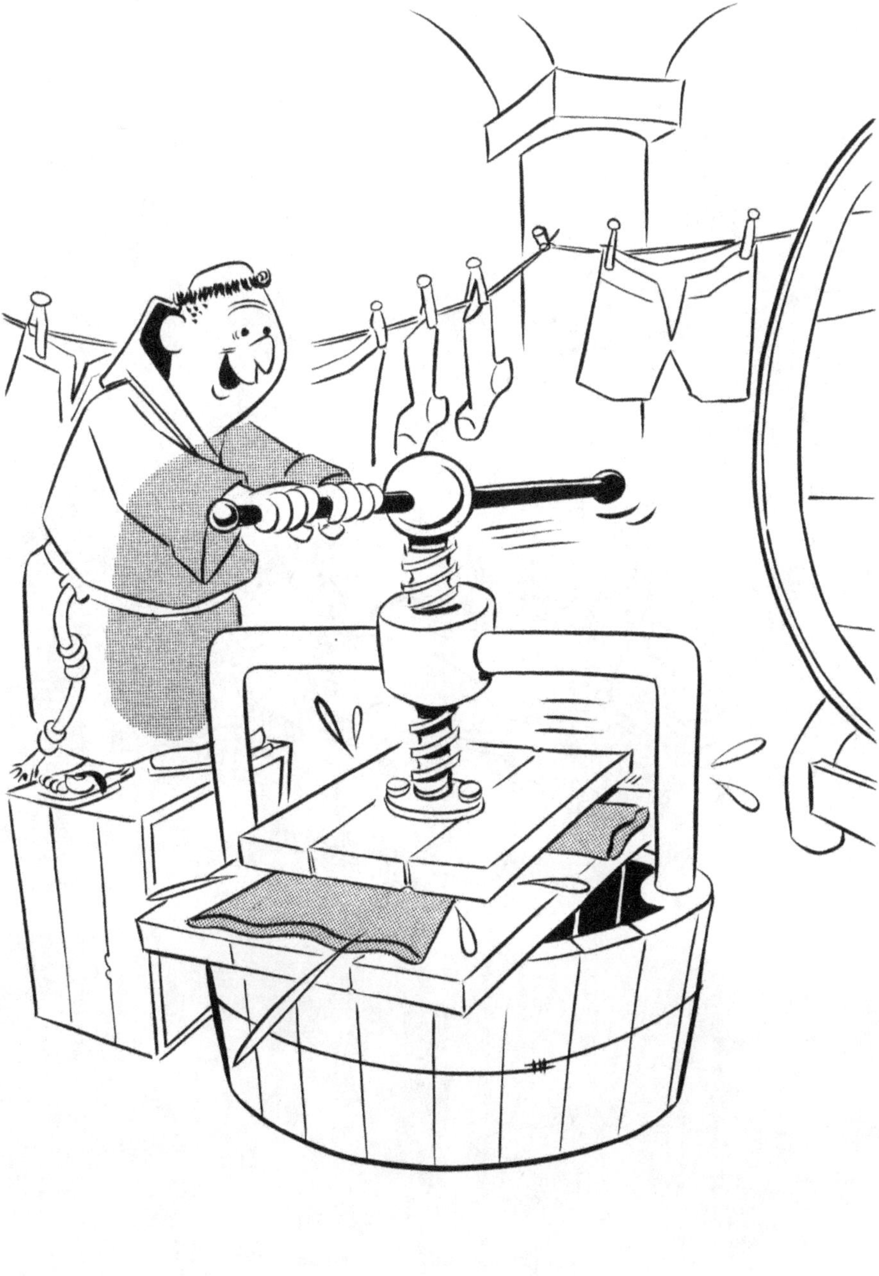

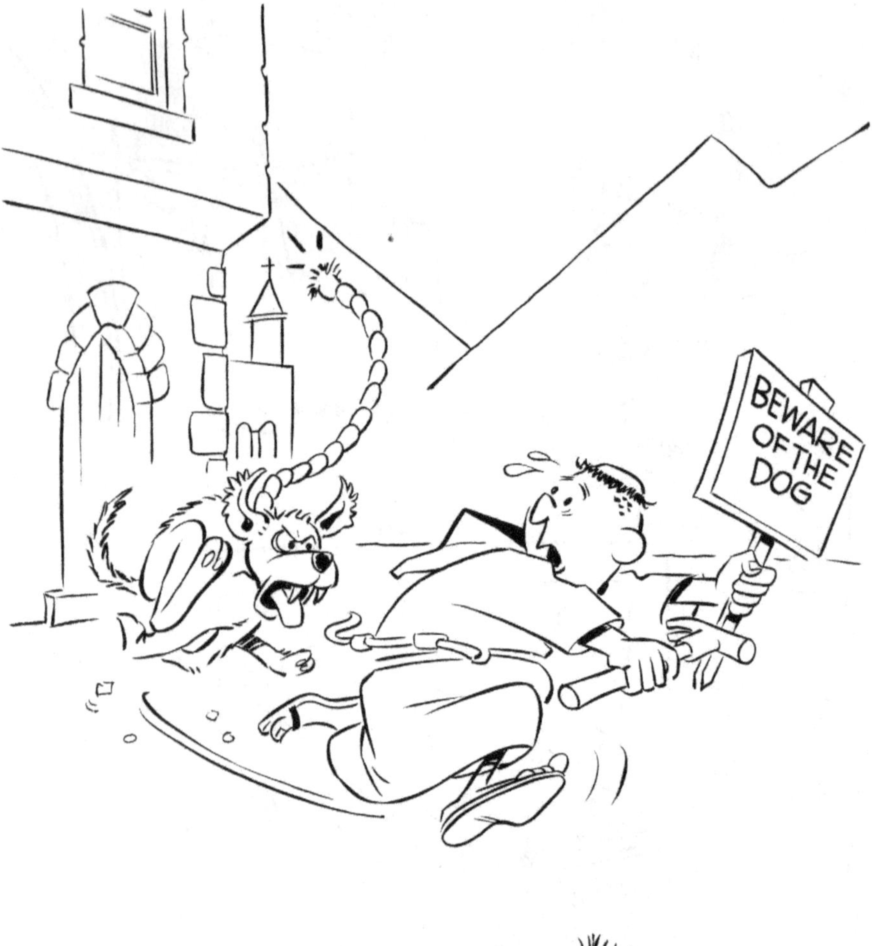
BEWARE OF THE DOG

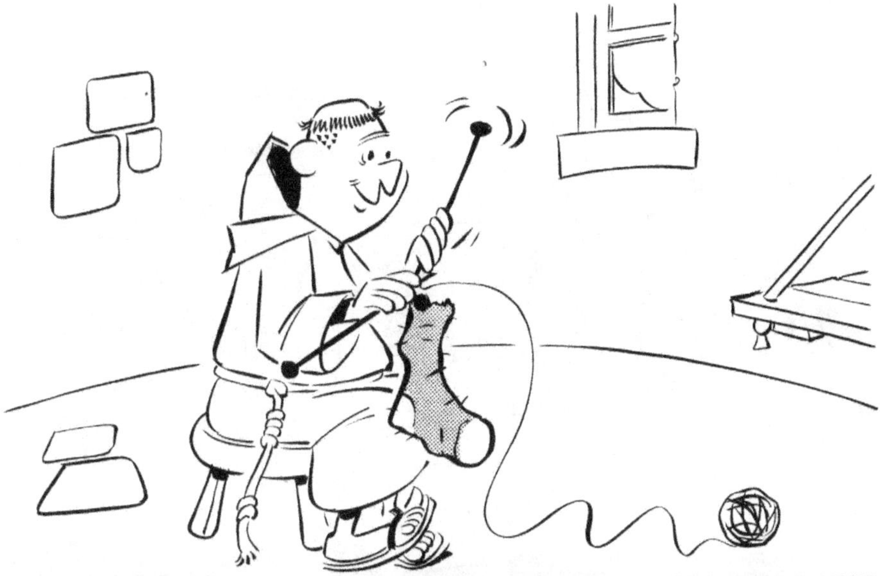

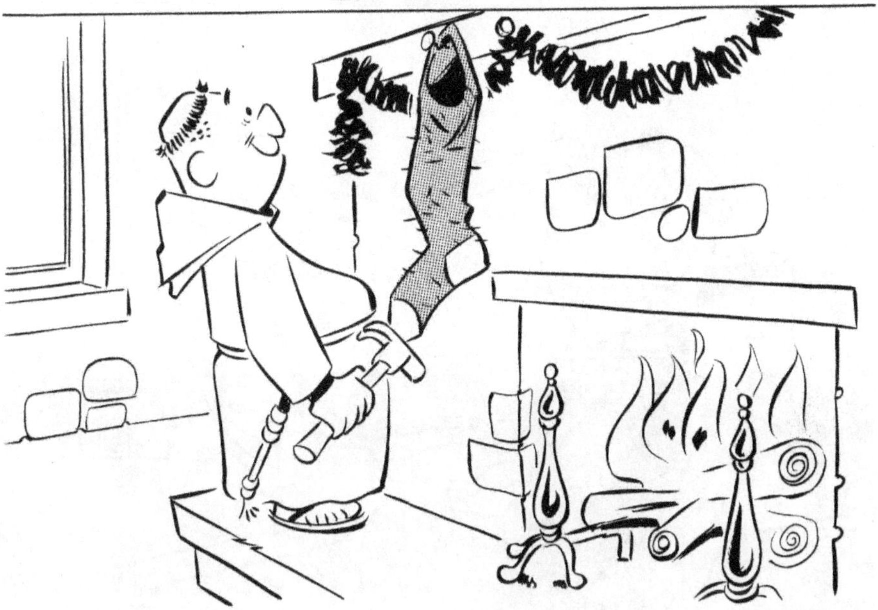

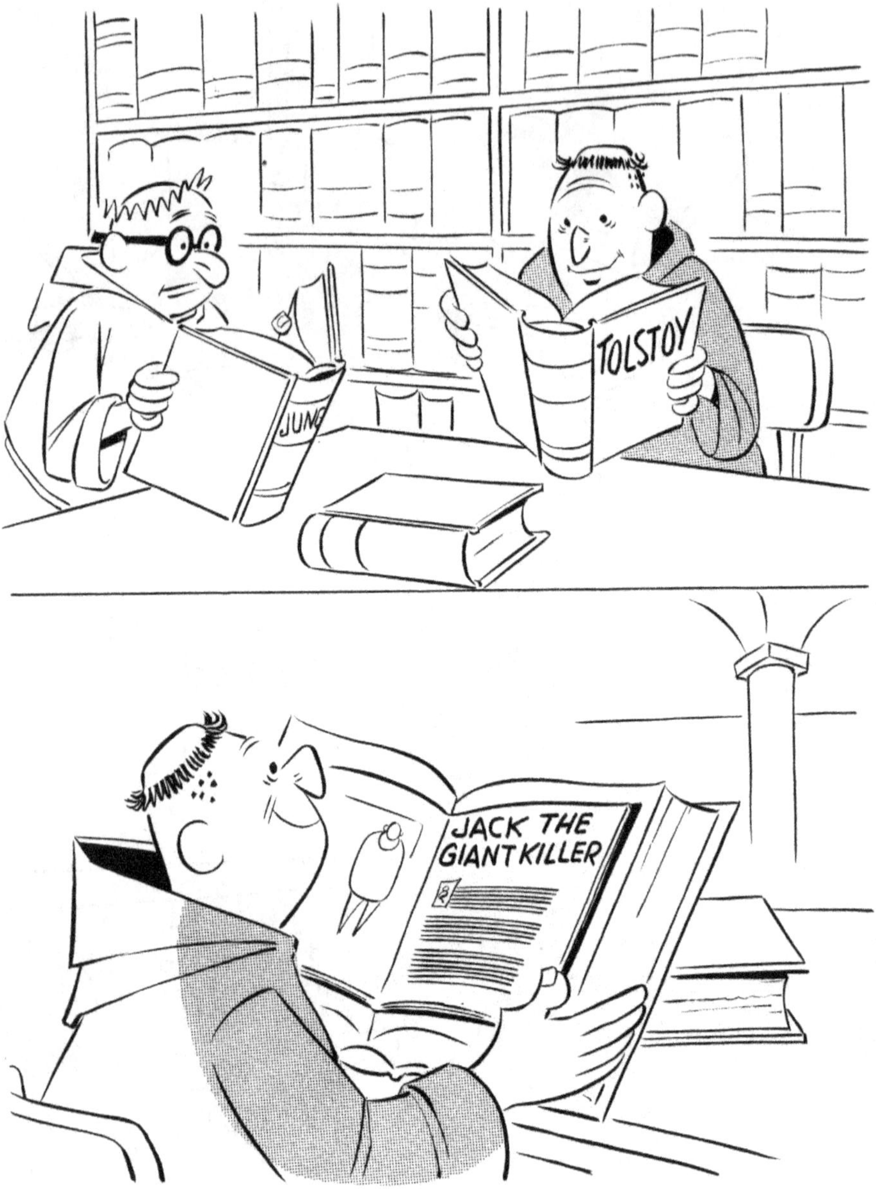
JUNG
TOLSTOY
JACK THE GIANT KILLER

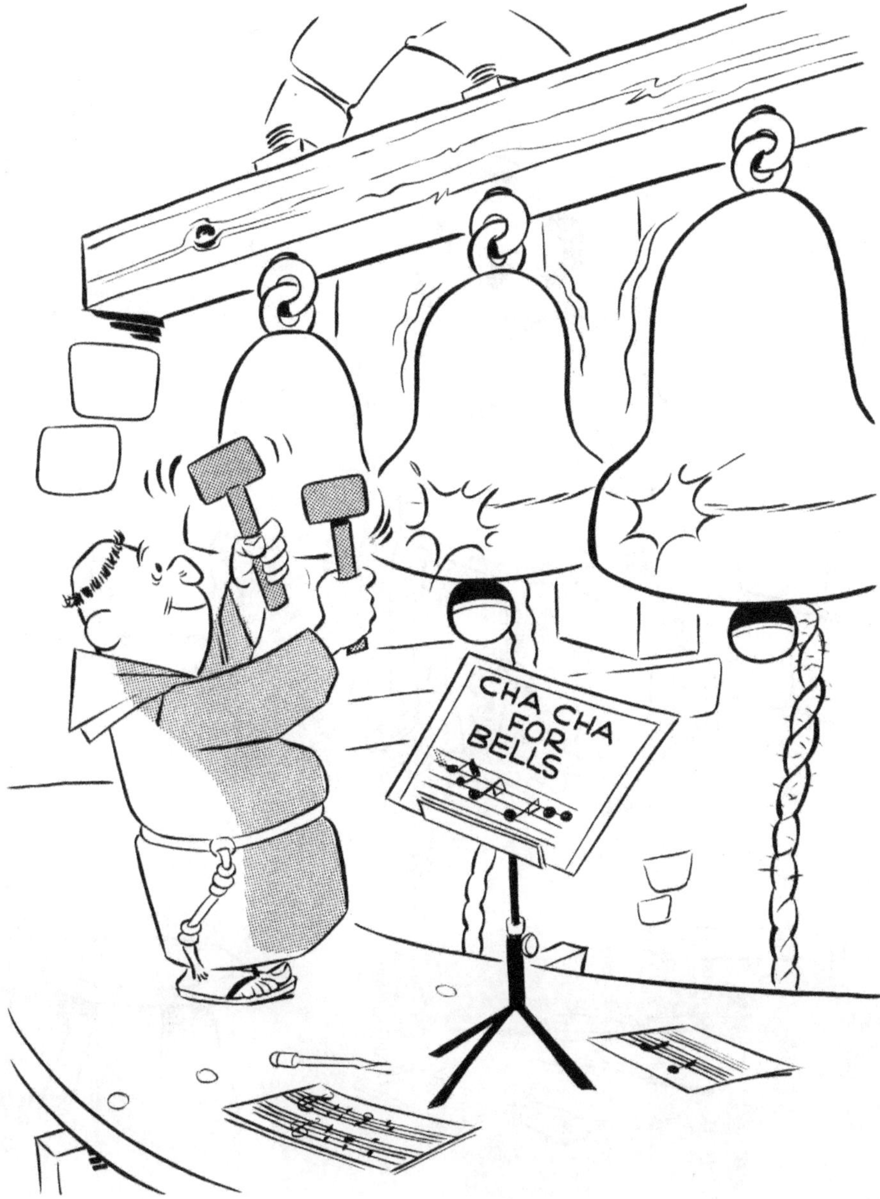
CHA CHA
FOR
BELLS

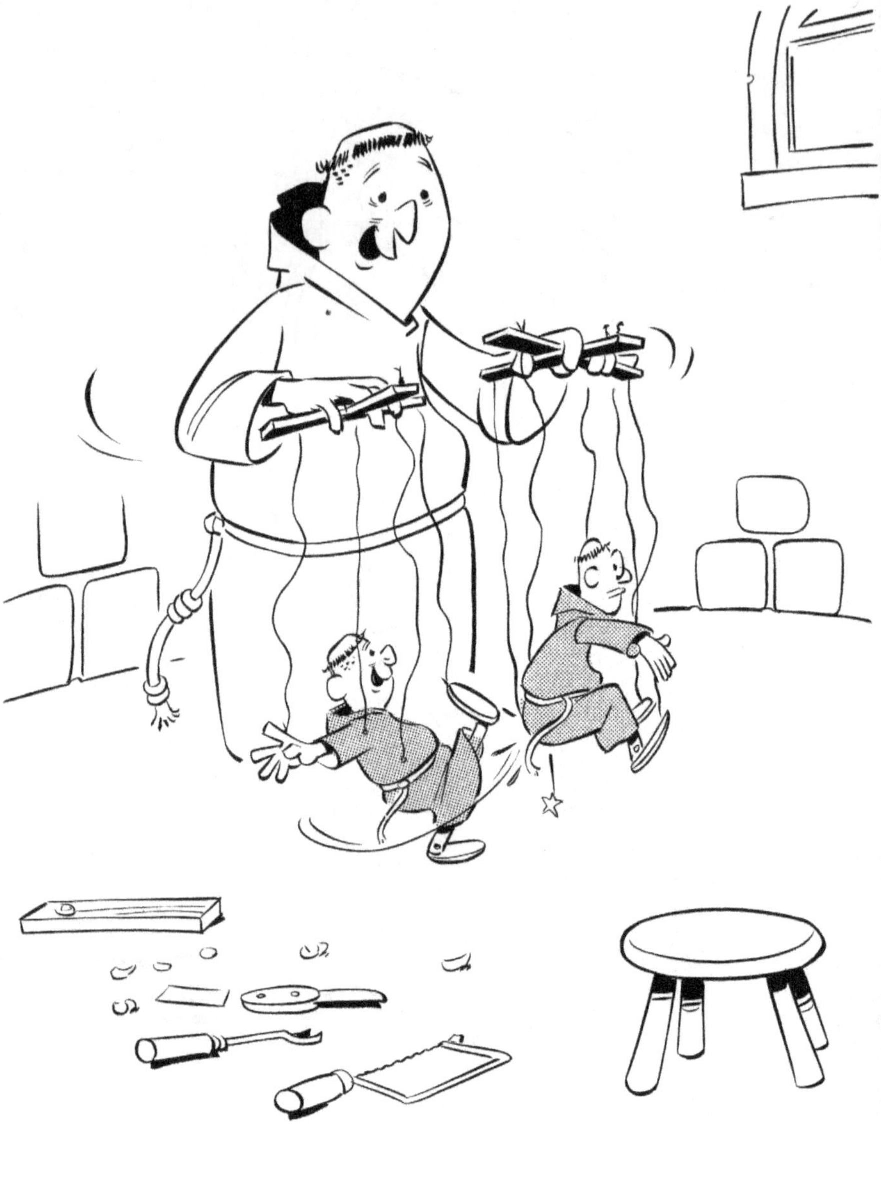

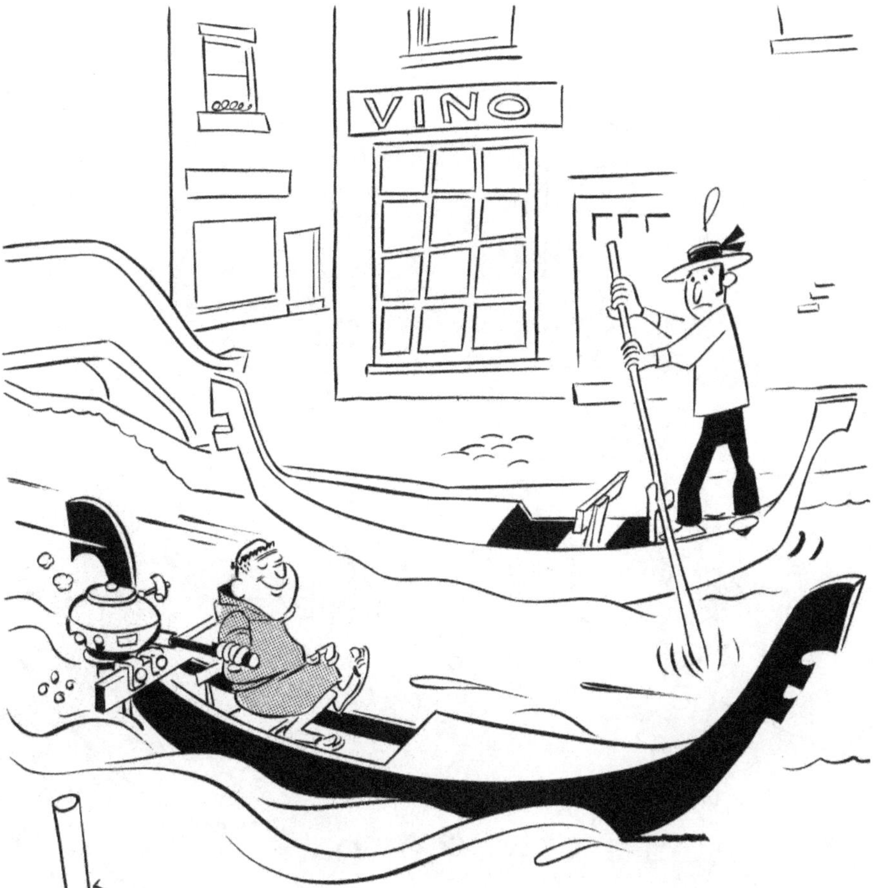
VINO

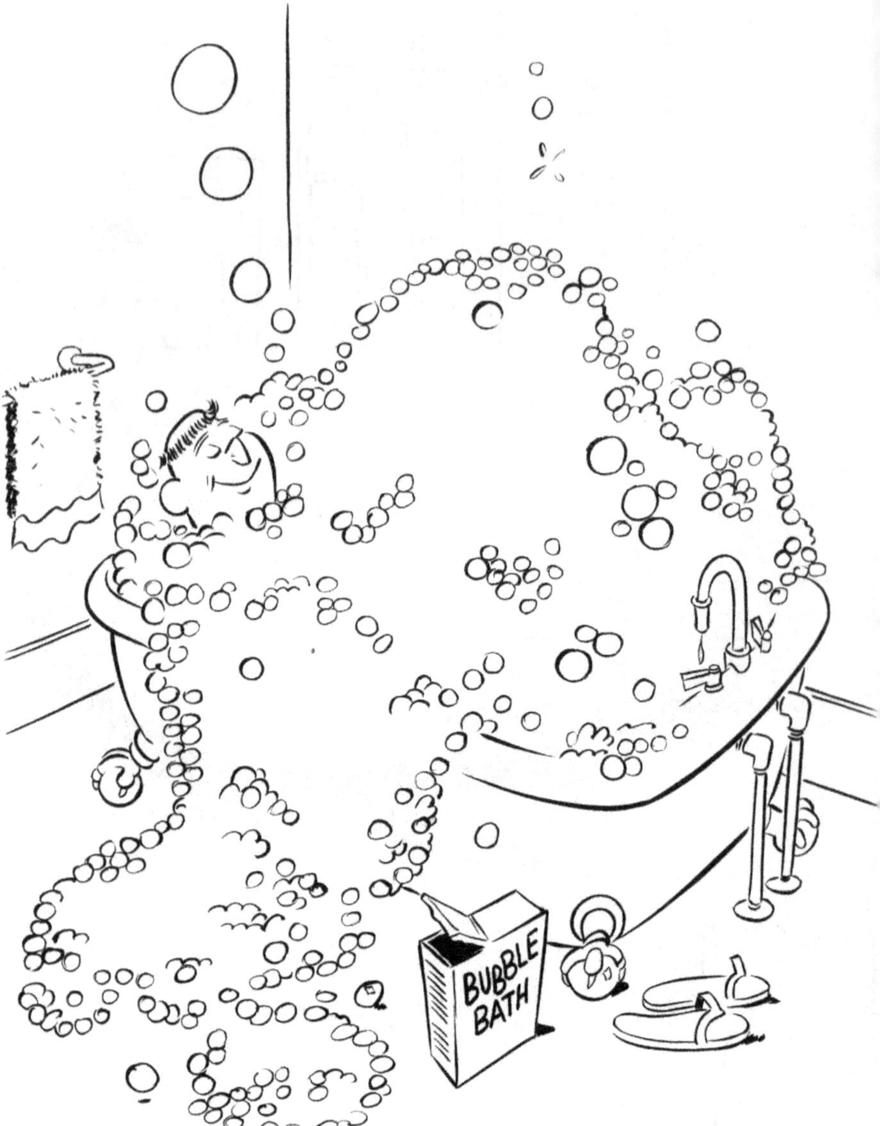
BUBBLE
BATH

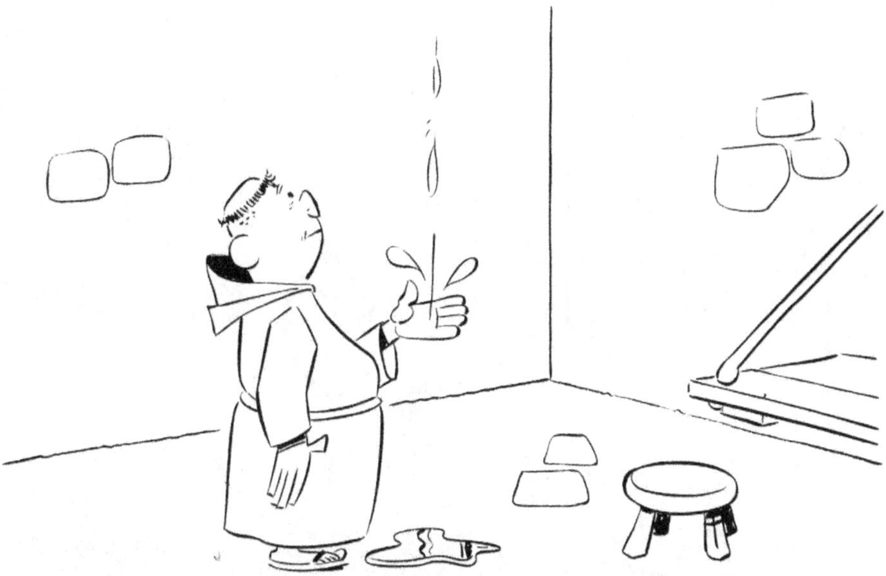

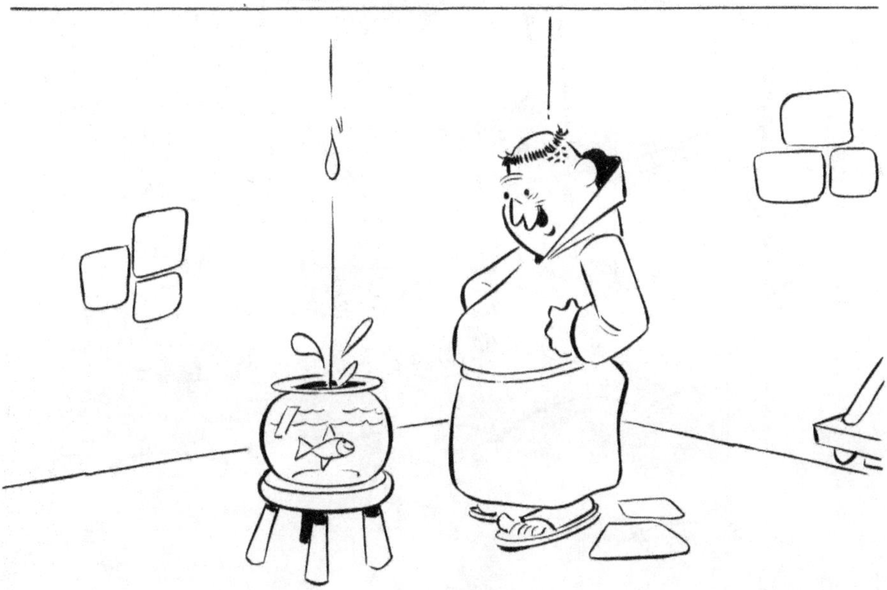

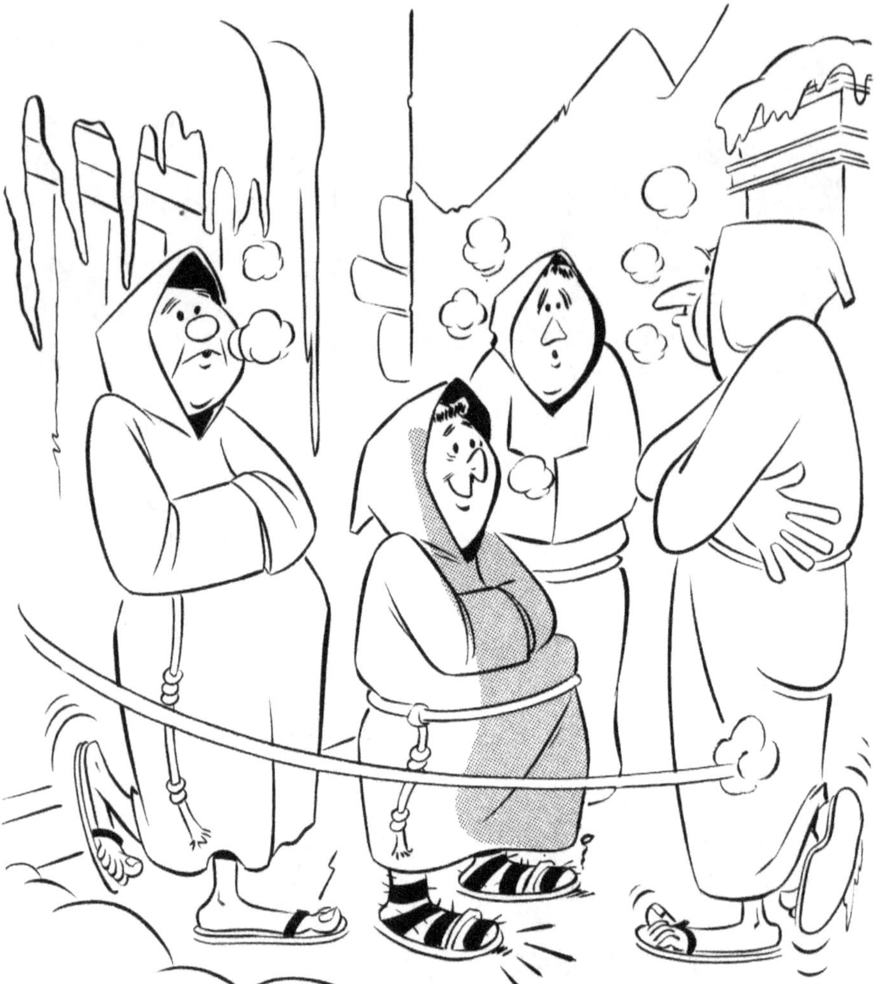

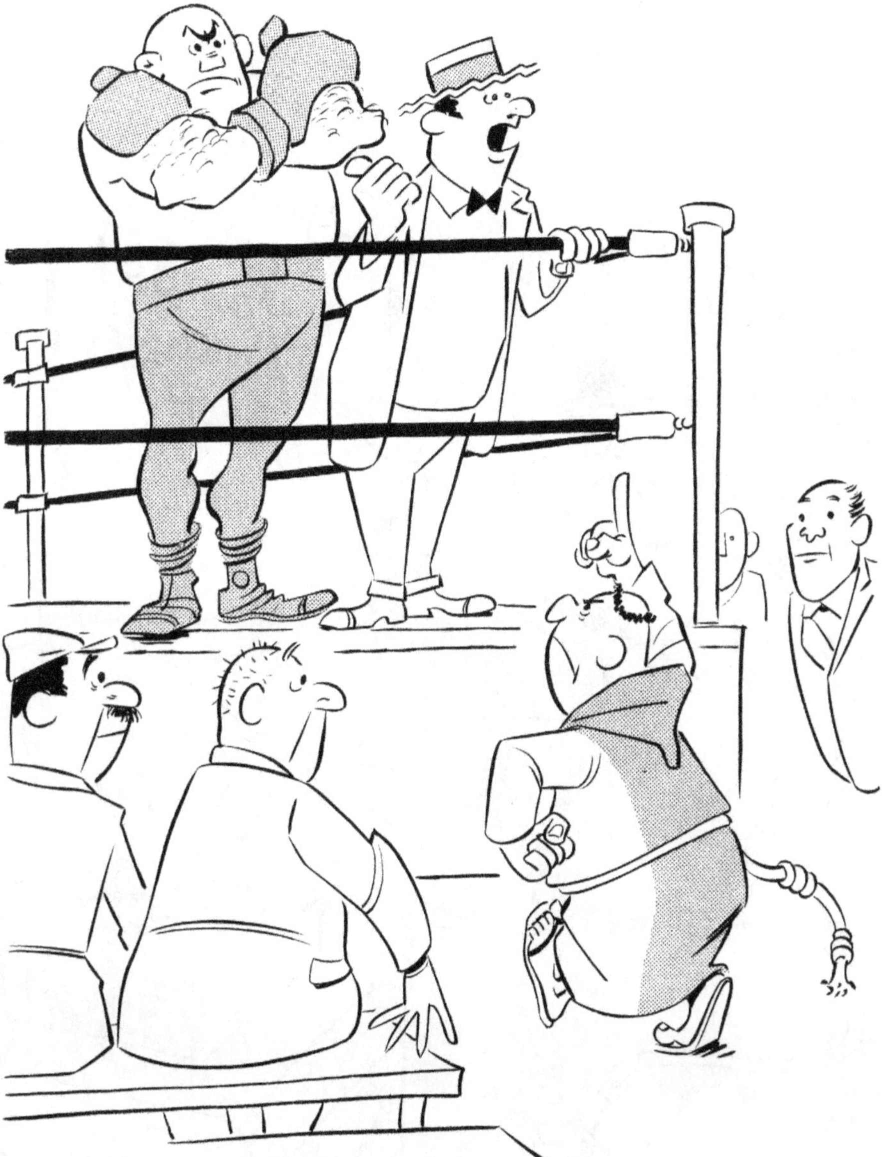

$100 to anyone staying 8 rounds with the mangler!

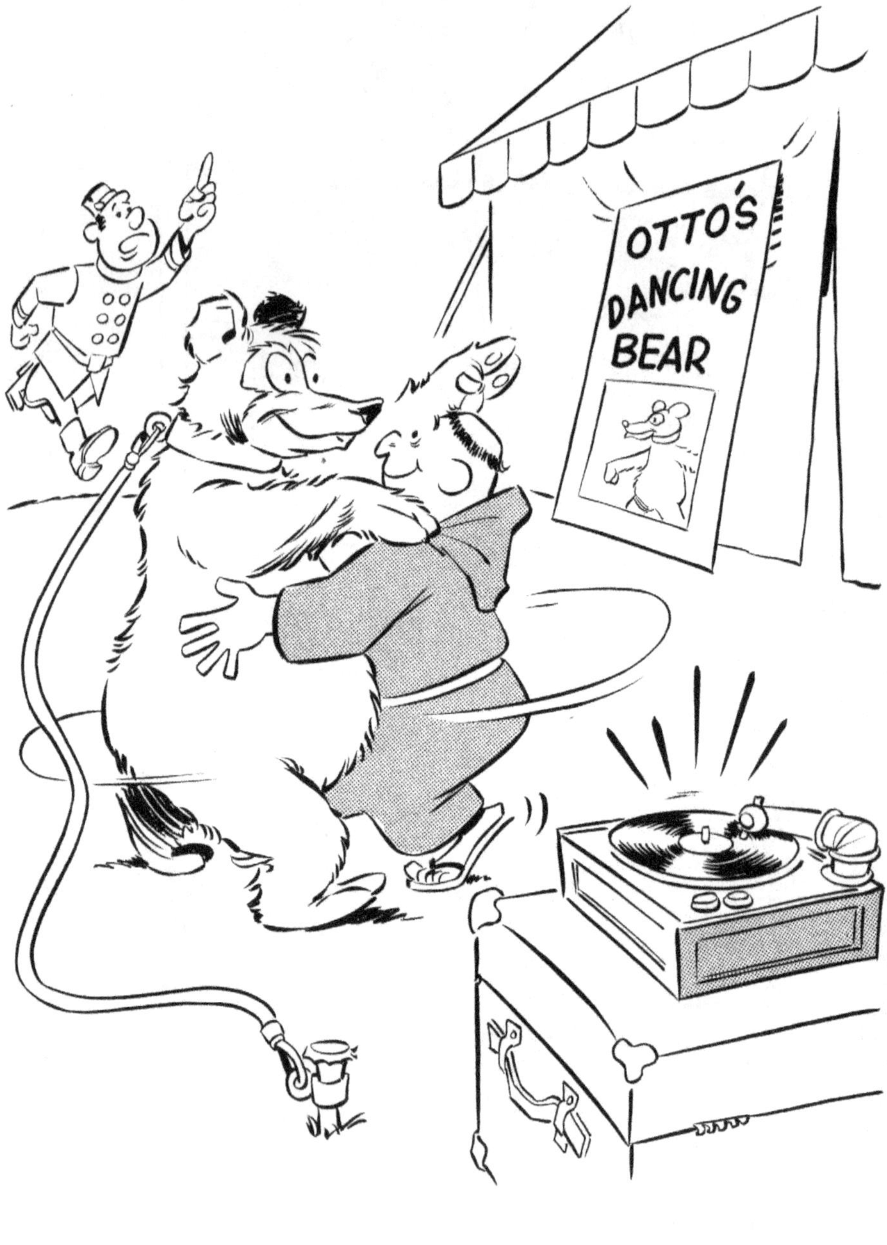
OTTO'S
DANCING
BEAR

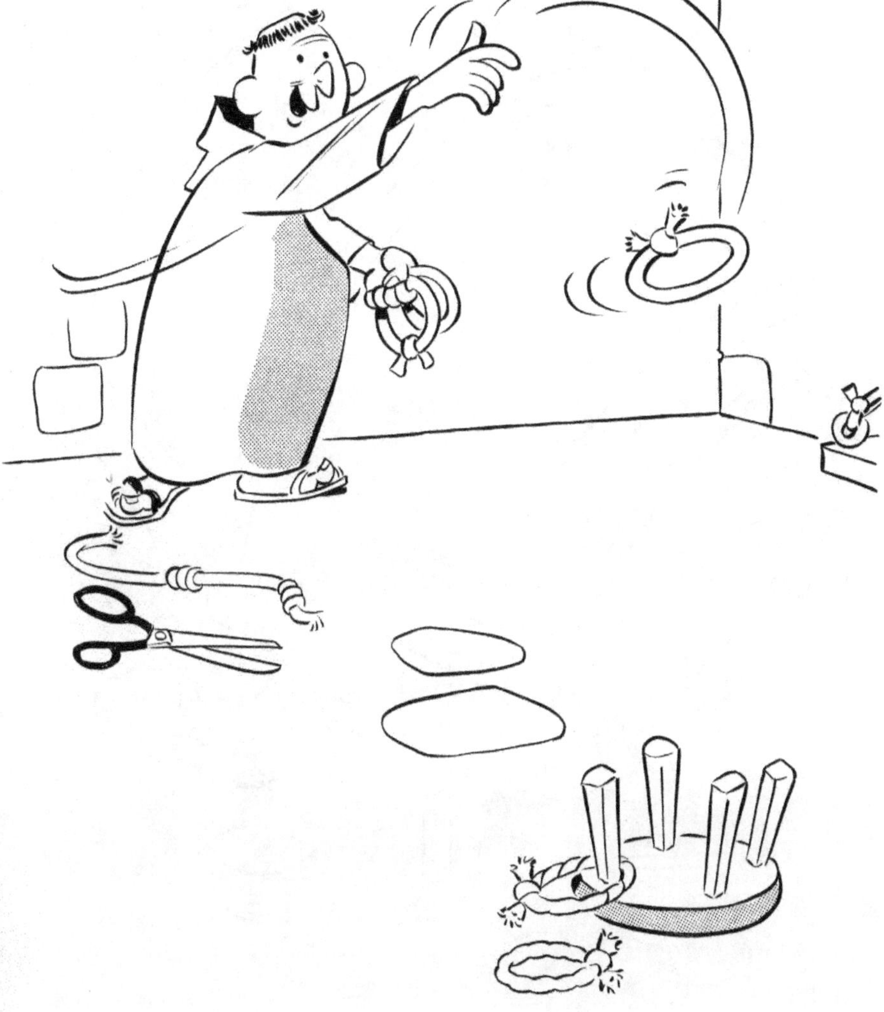

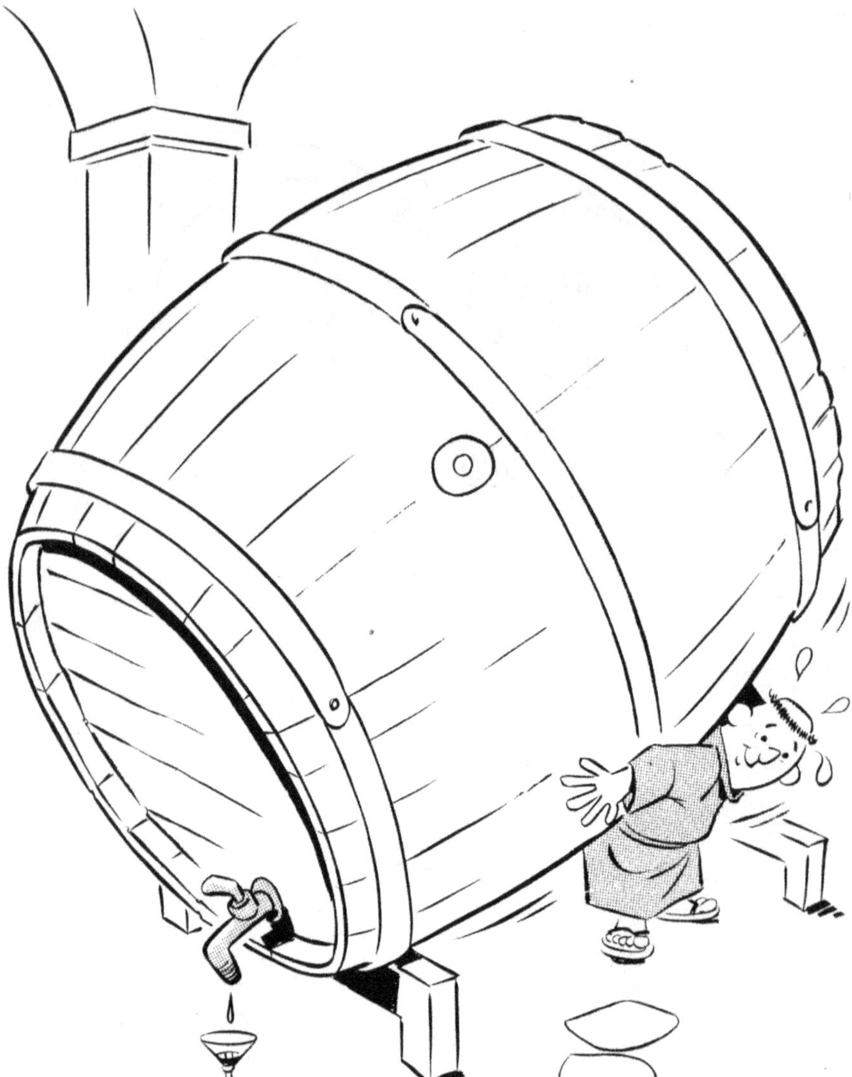

Also available...

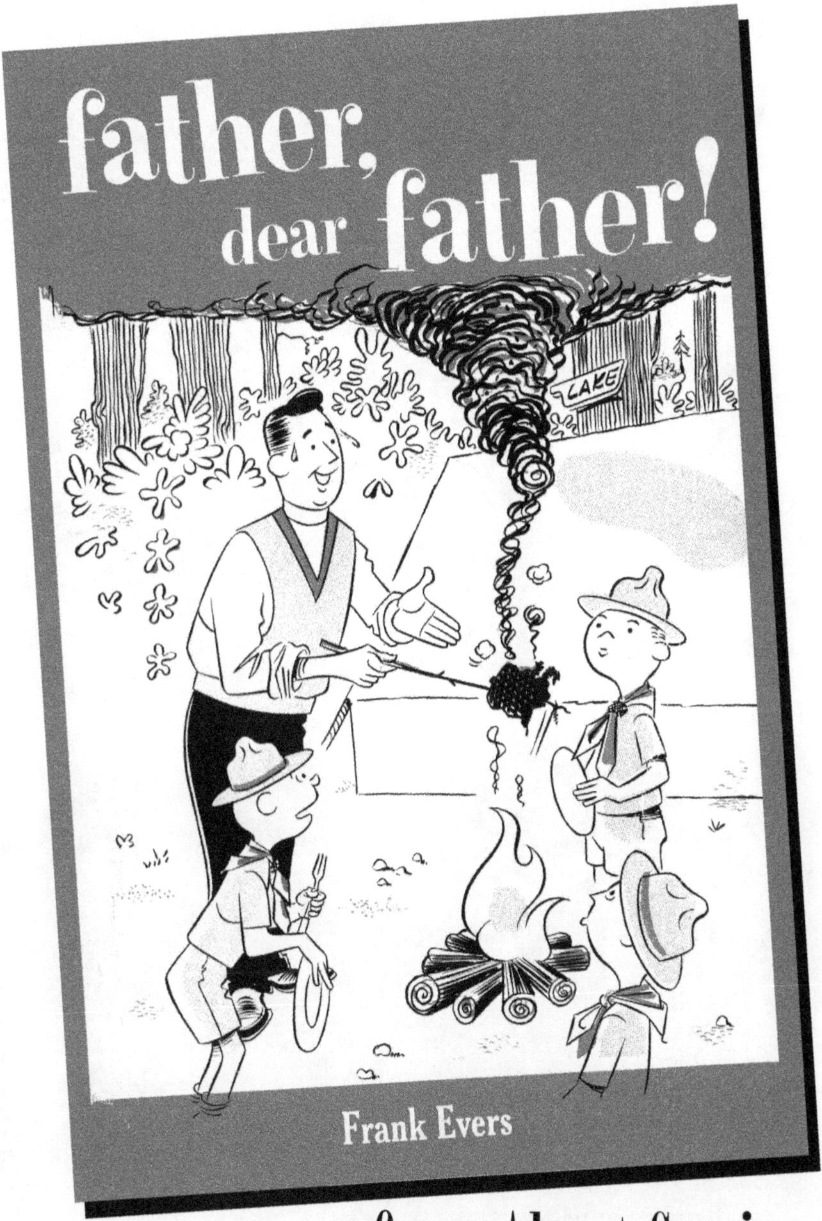

father, dear father!
LAKE
Frank Evers

... from About Comics

www.ingramcontent.com/pod-product-compliance
Lightning Source LLC
Chambersburg PA
CBHW021220020426
42331CB00003B/392